Learning to Program in
Visual
Basic .NET >>

S Langfield

Published by
PG Online Limited
The Old Coach House
35 Main Road
Tolpuddle
Dorset
DT2 7EW
United Kingdom
sales@pgonline.co.uk
www.pgonline.co.uk

PG ONLINE

Graphics: PG Online Ltd

Design and artwork: PG Online Ltd

First edition 2019

A catalogue entry for this book is available from the British Library

ISBN: 978-1-910523-18-6

Printed on FSC certified paper

Printed by Bell and Bain Ltd, Glasgow, UK.

Preface

Programming is fun! Trial and error is to be encouraged and you should type all of the examples and try all the exercises to get used to entering and debugging programs and to see how the programs run.

This book is intended for individuals and students who may have done some programming in other languages, but are not familiar with Visual Basic .NET. It is intended that users of the book should work through the book sequentially, starting at Chapter 1. However, it will be a useful reference book for students on a programming course or anyone working on a programming project.

It teaches basic syntax and programming techniques and introduces a number of useful features such as:

- **Developing graphical user interfaces** (GUIs) with the visual designer in Visual Studio.

- **SQLite**, which enables the creation and processing of a database from within a Visual Basic .NET program. This provides an alternative to writing to a text file when data needs to be stored and retrieved.

- **The Visual Studio debugger**, which can be used to help find elusive logic errors.

Questions and exercises are included throughout every chapter. Over 120 VB programs for all the examples and exercises given in the book may be downloaded from **www.pgonline.co.uk**. We strongly advise you to write your own code and check your solutions against the sample programs provided.

This book is a companion volume to the book Learning to Program in Python by P.M. Heathcote, and uses the same format. Questions and exercises from that text have been used throughout this book, with answers and programs rewritten in Visual Basic.

Enjoy – the sky's the limit!

Downloading Visual Basic .NET

VB.NET is a high-level programming language, implemented on the .NET Framework. Microsoft® launched VB.NET in 2002 as the successor to its original Visual Basic language. Microsoft's integrated development environment (IDE) for developing programs in VB.NET is called Visual Studio. Visual Studio Express and Visual Studio Community are freeware. VB.NET is available to be downloaded free from https://visualstudio. microsoft.com/vs/express/. The programs have been written and tested in Visual Studio Express 2019. Many schools and individuals may prefer to use alternative development environments and the book is equally applicable to these.

Contents

Chapter 1

Input, output and assignment

Objectives

- Write a simple console application

- Use string, numeric and Boolean data types and operators

- Learn the rules and guidelines for declaring and naming variables

- Use input and output statements

Programming in VB .NET

Visual Basic (VB) is a popular programming language. A VB program is simply a series of instructions written according to the rules or **syntax** of the language, usually designed to perform some task or come up with a solution to a problem. You write the instructions, and then the computer translates these instructions into binary machine code which the computer can execute. It will do this using a translator program, called a **compiler**.

VB.NET is the latest version of the Visual Basic programming language. It comes with an **integrated development environment** (IDE) which enables you to enter your program, save it, edit it, translate it to machine code and run it once it is free of syntax errors. If you have written a statement incorrectly, it will be reported by the IDE or the compiler as a syntax error, and you can correct it and try again.

You can write simple programs as a console application or you can write Windows® based applications using Windows forms (see Chapters 12 and 13).

Programming in VB.NET console mode

Launch Visual Studio and choose the **Create a new project** button in the **Get started** section:

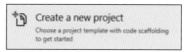

Next, select **Console App (.NET Framework)**. Other programming languages may be installed, so check that **Visual Basic** is given inside the button. If another language such as C# is given, then scroll through the list to find the Visual Basic version. Once the correct option button is selected click **Next**.

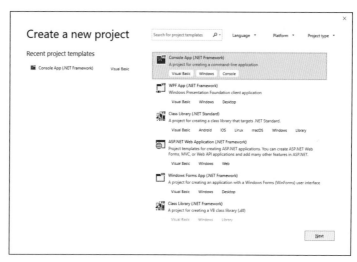

Choose the folder location where you want to save your programs. Then click **Create**.

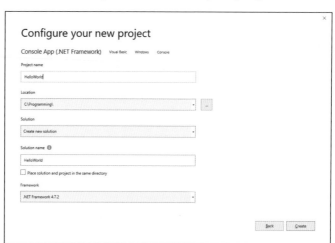

The IDE window now opens:

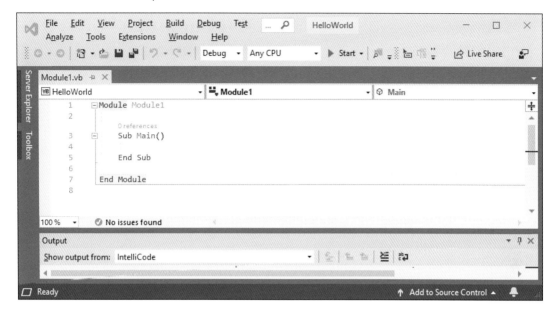

Type a one-line program:

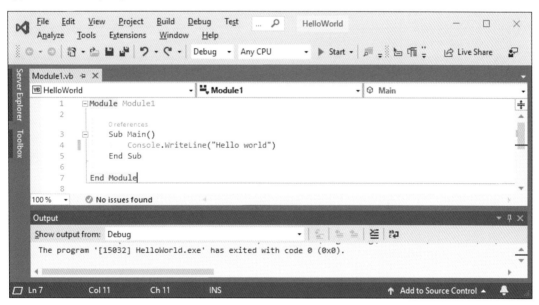

Click on the **Start** button ▶ Start ▾ on the IDE toolbar.

This starts the compiler. If there are no syntax errors the compiled program will then run.

The output will be shown in a separate console window.

Keeping the console window open

If you run the "Hello World" program, the program will run and then the console window will immediately close so that you can't see what happened. To keep it open, add these lines to your program:

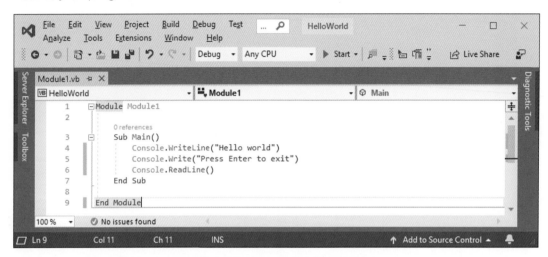

The window will remain open until the user presses the **Enter** key.

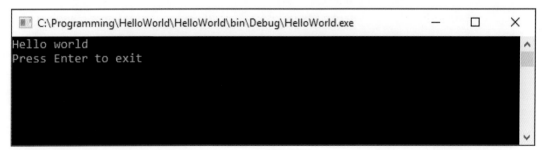

Adding comments

It's a good idea to include comments at the top of every program (beyond the very trivial) that you write, giving the name and purpose of the program, your name and the date you wrote the program. You may also want to document in which folder you have saved it so you can quickly find it again after a few weeks or months.

Within the program, add comments to document each function or procedure, and to explain the purpose of any tricky bits of code and how it works.

To write a comment, type the ' symbol. Anything to the right of ' will be ignored.

Programming conventions

- Write each statement on a separate line. Statements can be typed on the same line with a colon (:) as a separator. However, this is not recommended.

- The IDE will automatically indent your statements to make it easier to see which statements belong together.

Data types

String data type

In the previous programs, `"Hello World"` is a data type known as a **string**. A string is simply one or more characters enclosed in double quote marks. If your string contains speech or a quotation, you can use single quotes for this:

```
Console.Write("He said 'Hello!'")
```

produces the output:

```
He said 'Hello!'
```

The symbols + or & are used to **concatenate,** or join together, two strings.

```
Console.WriteLine("John" & " " & "Riddell")
```

produces the output:

```
John Riddell
```

Note that numbers enclosed in quotes behave as strings, not numbers. Therefore, both:

```
Console.WriteLine("7" & "3")     and
Console.WriteLine("7" + "3")
```

produce the output:

```
73
```

Numeric data types

A number can be either an **integer** (a whole number) or a **floating-point**, (a number with a decimal point) known in VB as **Integer** and **Single**, **Double** or **Decimal** respectively.

The standard arithmetic operators used by VB are +, −, * (multiply), / (divide) and ^ for exponentiation (e.g. 2^3 is written as $2\string^3$). The normal rules of precedence hold, and you can use parentheses to force the order of calculation. Two other useful operators are **Mod** and ****. Mod (meaning **modulus**) returns the remainder when one integer is divided by another, and \ (div in some languages) performs **integer division**.

So `19 Mod 5` = 4 and `19 \ 5` = 3.

Statement	Output
`Console.WriteLine(3 + 5 * 2)`	13
`Console.WriteLine((3 + 5) * 2)`	16
`Console.WriteLine(4 ^ 3)`	64
`Console.WriteLine(12 / 4)`	3
`Console.WriteLine(13 / 4)`	3.25
`Console.WriteLine(4.53 / 7.82)`	0.579283887468031
`Console.WriteLine(17 \ 6)`	2
`Console.WriteLine(17 Mod 6)`	5

Table 1.1

 Write statements to display the results of the following calculations:

(a) 10*6 + 5*3

(b) 10*(6 + 5)*3

(c) The remainder when 33 is divided by 7

Rounding a result

The result of `4.53 / 7.82` was shown as 0.579283887468031. To print an answer to a given number of decimal points, use the `Math.Round()` function.

```
Console.WriteLine(Math.Round((4.5 / 7.8), 2))
```

produces the output:

```
0.58
```

 Write statements to divide 6.7 by 3 and show the result to 3 decimal places.

Relational and logical operators

A **Boolean** data type can be either `True` or `False`. Operators fall into two categories: relational operators such as >, = (equals) and <> (not equal), and logical operators `And`, `Or` and `Not`.

The following table shows all the relational and logical operators.

Operation name	Operator
Less than	<
Greater than	>
Less than or equal	<=
Greater than or equal	>=
Equal	=
Not equal	<>
Logical and	And
Logical or	Or
Logical not	Not

Table 1.2: Relational and logical operators

Statement	Output
Console.WriteLine(18 = 6 * 3)	True
Console.WriteLine(18 = 6 / 3)	False
Console.WriteLine((5 > 2) And (7 > 6))	True
Console.WriteLine((6 < 8) Or (7 < 5))	True

Table 1.3

Note that extra spaces are used around operators in a statement to aid legibility.

Variables

When we want to store or change values we use **variables**. We name these so that we can refer to them later. The names are called identifiers or **variable names**.

Values are assigned to variables using the **assignment** operator (=).

Declaring and naming variables

Most programming languages require you to declare the type of data to be stored in a variable, so the correct amount of memory space can be reserved by the compiler. A variable declared to store an integer cannot then be used to store a string or the other way around. VB.NET requires variables to be declared before they are used.

```
Dim age As Integer
Dim name As String
Dim distance As Single 'This stores a 4-byte
                       'floating-point number
```

You can declare more than one variable of the same type on the same line.

```
Dim player1, player2, player3 As String
```

A valid variable name or identifier can contain only letters, numbers and the underscore character, and cannot start with a number. A variable is given a value using an **assignment statement**. The variable name is on the left-hand side of the assignment operator (=), and the value to be assigned is on the right-hand side.

```
Dim length As Integer
Dim width As Integer
length = 4
width = 3
Dim area As Integer = length * width
Dim perimeter As Integer = 2 * (length + width)
Console.WriteLine(area)
Console.WriteLine(perimeter)
Console.WriteLinee("Area = " & area)
```

produces the output:

```
12
14
Area = 12
```

Guidelines for naming variables

Using meaningful variable names will help you to create programs which are easy to follow, contain fewer errors and are easier for you or someone else to amend at a later date. Here are a few tips:

- Use the standard naming conventions for VB. Variable names should begin with a lowercase letter.

- Use meaningful, descriptive names; `length`, `width`, `area` rather than `x`, `y`, `z`.

- Don't make the names too long, and use **camel case** to separate parts of a name. For example, `passMark`, `maxMark`, `averageMark`.

- Note that variable names are not case-sensitive, so `AverageMark` and `averageMark` will be treated as the same variable. The IDE will automatically change these to match the first declared variable name.

> **Q3** Choose suitable variable names to create code for the following questions.
>
> (a) Assign the value 25 to the highest score in a game.
>
> (b) Assign the name Davina to a player.
>
> (c) Assign the values 4.5 and 6 to the height and base of a triangle. Calculate and print the area of the triangle, using the formula ½ (base x height).

Augmented assignment operators

These operators provide a shortcut to writing assignment statements.

Operator	Example	Equivalent to
+=	score += 1	score = score + 1
-=	score -= losses	score = score - losses
*=	score *= 2	score = score * 2
/=	score /= total	score = score / total
\=	score \= 7	score = score \ 7

Table 1.4: Augmented assignment operators

 Write statements using augmented assignment operators to do the following:

(a) Add 1 to counter.

(b) Double a variable called housePrice.

(c) Subtract a variable called penalty from a variable called hits.

(d) Divide totalCostOfMeal by 3.

The Write and WriteLine statements

You have already seen the Console.Write and Console.WriteLine statements used to display text on the screen.

Using an ampersand (&) as a concatenation operator

You can use **&** to separate strings or variables:

```
Dim length As Integer = 15
Console.WriteLine("The length is " & length & " metres")
```

produces the output:

```
The length is 15 metres
```

Using & has the advantage that you do not have to worry about the variable type. You can mix integers, real numbers and strings in the Write statement.

Using + as a concatenation operator

Instead of using &, you can use a + operator to concatenate strings in the output. However, you cannot join a string to an integer or real number, so you first have to convert any numbers to strings.

The following program causes an InvalidCastException error as the String cannot be converted to a number.

```
Dim cost As Integer = 15
Console.WriteLine ("The cost is £" + cost)
```

To convert a number to a string, you use the `Str()` function. This is discussed in more detail in the next chapter. (See *Converting between strings and numbers on page 18.*)

```
Console.WriteLine ("The cost is £" + Str(cost))
```

produces the output:

```
The cost is £ 15
```

To remove the space, use the `CStr()` function:

```
Console.WriteLine ("The cost is £" + CStr(cost))
```

Inserting a new line or tab

vbCrLf (Carriage return, Line feed) and vbTab are used to make a new line and a tab.

Statement	Output
`Console.WriteLine (vbCrLf & "Hello")`	Hello
`Console.` `WriteLine (vbCrLf & "Goodbye" & vbCrLf)`	Goodbye

`Console.`
`WriteLine ("x" & vbTab & "x squared")`
`Console.WriteLine ("3" & vbTab & "9")`
`Console.WriteLine ("10" & vbTab & "100")`
	x x squared
	3 9
	10 100

Printing two outputs on the same line

To avoid printing on a new line, use `Write` instead of the `WriteLine` statement, so for example:

```
Console.WriteLine ("This should all print ")
Console.WriteLine ("on the same line")
```

produces the output:

```
This should all print on the same line
```

(a) Write a statement to display "More pain, more gain".

(b) Write a statement to display "That's true!".

(c) Write a statement to concatenate two strings "Pelham" and "123" and display the result.

(d) What will be displayed when you enter the following on three lines?

```
Console.WriteLine("How will this " &
            "statement " &
        "be printed?")
```

Try it out.

Writing a multi-line statement

The last question demonstrates that you can split a statement over several lines.

```
Console.WriteLine("This is a long line of text
split in the middle of the quote")
```

produces the output:

```
This is a long line of text
split in the middle of the quote
```

```
Console.WriteLine("
John Smith
23 Elm Street
Andover
")
```

produces the output:

```
John Smith
23 Elm Street
Andover
```

Outside quote marks, additional spaces between variables or operators are ignored.

The ReadLine statement

The ReadLine statement is used to accept input from the user and assign the input to a variable on the left-hand side of an assignment statement.

1

```
Dim firstName, surname As String
Console.WriteLine("Please enter your first name: ")
firstName = Console.ReadLine()
Console.WriteLine("Please enter your surname: ")
surname = Console.ReadLine()
Console.WriteLine("Full name is " & firstName & " " & surname)
```

produces the output:

```
Please enter your first name: Martha
Please enter your surname: Harris
Full name is Martha Harris
```

Mixing strings and variables in a Write statement

You can use the & sign to include a variable in a `Write` statement. Extending the above program with:

```
Console.WriteLine(firstName & ", " & "please enter your
                   phone number: ")
Dim phoneNumber As String = Console.ReadLine()
```

produces the output:

```
Martha, please enter your phone number:
```

There is no need to convert any numbers to strings if you use & symbols:

```
Dim answer3 As String
Dim question As Integer = 3
Console.WriteLine("Enter the answer to question " &
                   question & ": ")
answer3 = Console.ReadLine()
```

```
Enter the answer to question 3:
```

(program then waits for the user to enter data).

Exercises

1. (a) Write statements to prompt a user to input their favourite food and favourite colour and display this information in the format "My favourite food is xxxx and my favourite colour is yyyy", using + operators to concatenate the separate strings.

    (b) Display the same information using the & operator instead of + operators.

2. (a) Write statements to ask the user to enter their name and telephone number and then print this information on two separate lines, with a blank line in between.

    (b) Print the name and telephone number on the same line, separated by a tab.

3. Write statements to:

    (a) perform the integer division of 40 by 11

    (b) find the remainder when 40 is divided by 11

    (c) calculate 2^{10}

    (d) test whether "three" is greater than "two"

    (e) test whether "abc" is less than "ABC"

    (f) test whether (1 <= 4 and 7 <= 7) is True

    (g) find the result of the Boolean condition equivalent to: "Fred" not equal to "fred"

1

Chapter 2
Strings and numbers

Objectives

- Learn some useful string methods and functions
- Convert string input to numerical values and vice versa
- Identify and correct syntax errors
- Use named constants

String functions

We can alter and find out information about strings by using built-in string functions. A **function** is written with the function name followed by the name of the `string` and any other arguments required in brackets.

Function	Example	Description
UCase	`UCase(aString)`	returns `aString` all in uppercase
LCase	`LCase(aString)`	returns `aString` all in lowercase
InStr	`InStr(aString, bString)`	returns the position of the first occurrence of `bString` in `aString`, or 0 if not found
Replace	`Replace(aString,oldStr, newStr)`	replaces all occurrences of `oldStr` substring with `newStr` in `aString`
Len	`Len(aString)`	Returns the length (number of characters) in `aString`

Table 2.1: String functions

Every character in a string may be referred to by its **index** number in the string. The first character in a string `myString` is referred to as `myString(0)`. Most other languages, such as C# and Python, also use 0 to index the first character in a string.

However, note that the function `InStr` numbers the character positions from 1 not 0. So when you want to find the position using the InStr function, you need to decrease the returned result by 1 (see example 1 below).

Finding the length of a string

The example below shows a useful function to find the number of characters in a string:

```
numChars = Len(aString)
```

Below is a program which uses some of the string functions. All the programs given in the text as examples and exercises may be downloaded from **www.pgonline.co.uk**.

Example 1

```
'Program name: Ch 2 Example 1 String methods
'Tests String methods
Dim aString As String
aString = "You've done a good job"
Console.WriteLine("Original string: " & aString)
Console.WriteLine("The string length is: " & Len(aString))
Console.WriteLine("Uppercase string: " & UCase(aString))
Console.Write("New String: ")
Console.WriteLine(Replace(aString, "good", "brilliant"))
Console.WriteLine("Original string: " & aString)
Console.WriteLine("The word 'done' starts at index ")
Console.WriteLine(InStr(aString, "done") - 1)
```

When you run the program, the output appears in the console window:

```
Original string: You've done a good job
The string length is: 22
Uppercase string: YOU'VE DONE A GOOD JOB
New String: You've done a brilliant job
Original string: You've done a good job
The word 'done' starts at index 7
```

Notice that the original string is left unchanged. If you want to save the changed string, you could write, for example:

```
bString = UCase(aString)
```

or:

```
aString = UCase(aString)
```

Syntax errors

If you make any mistakes when entering statements, the computer will report a syntax error.

Example 2

Some errors have been inserted into the program in Example 1.

The IDE checks programming code as it is entered. As soon as it encounters a syntax error, it will underline it with a red wriggly line.

```
'Program name: Ch 2 Example 1 String methods
'Tests String methods
Dim aString As String
aString = "You've done a good job"
Console.WriteLine("Original string: " aString)
                                    ┌─────────────────────────────────────────────────┐
                                    │ Comma, ')', or a valid expression continuation expected. │
                                    └─────────────────────────────────────────────────┘
Console.WriteLine("The string length is: " & Le(aString)
```

When you hover the mouse pointer over the area containing the error, the IDE will suggest what is wrong. For example, the first error above gives the suggestion:

> Comma, ')', or a valid expression continuation expected.

The suggestion is not always very clear. Here, there is a missing & before the variable name aString.

 Q1 There are two more errors in the program, shown by the red wiggly underlines. Explain what is wrong in each case.

Numbers

There are many different data types that are used in VB to store numbers. The key ones are given in the table below.

Numeric data type	Memory required	Used for
Single	2 bytes	Floating point numbers
Integer	4 bytes	A 32 bit integer from: -2,147,483,648 to 2,147,483,647
Double	8 bytes	Floating-point numbers – twice the accuracy of Single
Decimal	16 bytes	Very accurate floating-point numbers – up to 28 decimal places

Table 2.2: Numeric data types

Inputting numbers

A simple program to find the cost of lunch is shown below.

Example 3

```
'Program name: Ch 2 Example 3 Cost Of lunch
Dim mainMeal, juice, banana, total As Decimal
mainMeal = 3.0
juice = 0.75
banana = 1.0
total = mainMeal + juice + banana
Console.WriteLine("Total for lunch: " & Total)
```

This prints out

```
Total for lunch: 4.75
```

Example 4

To make the program more useful, we could ask the user to enter the cost of the main course, juice and banana. Here is a first attempt:

```
'Program name: Ch 2 Example 4 Cost Of lunch
Dim mainMeal, juice, banana, total As Decimal
Console.Write("Enter cost of main course: ")
mainMeal = Console.ReadLine()
Console.Write("Enter cost of juice: ")
juice = Console.ReadLine()
Console.Write("Enter cost of banana: ")
banana = Console.ReadLine()
total = mainMeal + juice + banana
Console.WriteLine("Total for lunch: " & total)
```

When you run this program, the output is:

```
Enter cost of main course: 4.00
Enter cost of juice: 0.50
Enter cost of banana: 1
Total for lunch: 5.50
```

`Console.Readline` will automatically convert the input to the data type of the variable it is assigned to. So if the variable is declared as an integer and the input is a real number, then VB rounds to the next whole number.

2

Converting between strings and numbers

There may be occasions when you wish to convert from `String` to `Integer`, `Single`, `Decimal` or `Double`. Here are some useful conversion functions:

Function	Description	Example	Returns
CDbl(x)	converts a string to a floating-point value of type Double	`CDbl("4.65")`	`4.65`
CDec(x)	converts a string to a floating-point value of type Decimal	`CDec("4.65")`	`4.65`
CSng(x)	converts a string to a floating-point value of type Single	`CSng ("4.65")`	`4.65`
Cint(x)	converts a string to an integer	`Cint("3")`	`3`
CStr(x)	Converts a number x to a string value	`CStr(5.0)`	`"5.0"`

Table 2.3: Type conversion functions

Example 5

The formatting of output is covered in Chapter 9, pages 75-77. An explanation is left until then; however, if you change the last line of the program in Example 4 to:

```
Console.WriteLine("Total for lunch: {0:C}", total)
```

then the variable `Total` will appear as currency:

```
Total for lunch: £5.50
```

Functions and methods

The string data type in VB.NET is an **object**. Strings have built-in **methods** which perform useful tasks. Instead of the functions from Table 2.1, the string methods shown in Table 2.4 can be used.

Method	Example	Description
ToUpper	`aString.ToUpper()`	returns `aString` all in uppercase
ToLower	`aString.ToLower()`	returns `aString` all in lowercase
IndexOf	`aString.IndexOf(item)`	returns the index of the first occurrence of `Item` in `aString`, or -1 if not found
Replace	`aString.Replace(oldStr,newStr)`	replaces all occurrences of `oldStr` substring with `newStr` in `aString`

Table 2.4: String methods

Note the different ways in which functions and methods are written. A **method** is written using dot notation, with the name of the object followed by a full-stop and then the method name:

```
posA = aString.IndexOf("A")
```

Constants

When we use values that never change throughout the program, such as the mathematical constant π (3.14159), we can declare this as a constant at the beginning of the program.

```
Const Pi = 3.14159
```

The advantage of declaring a value as a constant rather than a variable is that the value can't be accidentally changed within the program. Using a named constant in programming statements rather than the actual value makes the program statements easier to follow. Also, if the value needs to be changed (for example if we want to use π accurate to more decimal places) we only need to change the value at the beginning of the program.

Exercises

1. Write a program to do the following:

    *   assign the string "A picture's worth a thousand words" to `proverb`.

    *   replace "A picture's" with "An image is" and assign the new string to `proverbImage`.

    *   find the first occurrence of the letter "o" in the original string and assign the value of the index to `firstO`.

    *   convert the original string to uppercase and assign it to `proverbUpper`.

    *   find the number of characters in the string.

    *   display the results of all these operations, as well as the original string.

2. Write a program to ask the user to enter the radius of a circle and print out the area, πr^2 and the circumference, $2\pi r$. (π = 3.14159).

3. Write a program which asks the user to type in two floating-point numbers `num1` and `num2`, then rounds and prints their sum and product to the specified number of decimal places:

    ```
    The sum of num1 and num2 is nnnn.nn
    The product of num1 and num2 is nnnn.nnn
    ```

    For example:

    ```
    The sum of 3.453 and 2.1 is 5.55
    The product of 3.453 and 2.1 is 7.251
    ```

2

Chapter 3

Selection

Objectives

- Learn to write conditional statements using Boolean expressions
- Write selection statements using `If, Else, ElseIf`
- Use nested if statements
- Use complex Boolean expressions involving `And, Or` and `Not`
- Use the `Rnd()` function or `Random` object to create random numbers

Programming constructs

There are three basic ways of controlling the order in which program statements are carried out:

Sequence, **selection** and **iteration**.

In the previous two chapters, you wrote program statements one after the other in the order in which they were to be executed. This is the **sequence** programming construct.

This chapter uses **selection** statements to control program flow. These statements all start with the keyword `If`, followed by a condition to be tested. For example:

```
If shape = "circle" Then
    area = Pi * r ^ 2
Else
    area = length * breadth
End If
```

The IDE will automatically indent the statements between `If` and `Else` and between `Else` and `End If`.

Note that the = symbol means 'equal to' here but it is also used with variables when it means 'assign' a value to the variable.

Boolean conditions

The following **Boolean operators** may be used in `If` statements:

=	equal to
<>	not equal to
>	greater than
>=	greater than or equal to
<	less than
<=	less than or equal to

Table 3.1: Boolean operators

 Q1 Write statements to input two numbers and assign the smaller of the two to a variable called `minimum`.

Using a Boolean variable in a condition statement

A **Boolean variable** can only take the value `True` or `False`. So, for example, we could write a conditional statement such as:

```
If amount < 10 Then
    validAmount = True
End If
```

and later in the program, the Boolean variable `validAmount` could be tested with the statement:

```
If validAmount = True Then
    Console.WriteLine("This is a valid amount")
End If
```

However, the statement can also be written more simply as:

```
If validAmount Then
    Console.WriteLine("This is a valid amount")
End If
```

The `ElseIf` clause

This is useful if there are several possible routes through the program depending on the value of a variable.

3

Example 1

Students are assigned a grade of A, B, C or F depending on the average mark they have achieved over a number of assignments.

Mark of 75 or more: A
Mark of 60 – 74:   B
Mark of 50 – 59:   C
Mark less than 50:   F

The following shows how a grade can be assigned to a variable called `grade` depending on the value of `mark`.

```
If mark >= 75 Then
    grade = "A"
ElseIf mark >= 60 Then
    grade = "B"
ElseIf mark >= 50 Then
    grade = "C"
Else
    grade = "F"
End If
```

A particular `ElseIf` is tested only when all previous `If` and `ElseIf` statements are False. When one `If` or `ElseIf` statements is True, all subsequent tests are skipped.

Case statements

Example 2

If there is more than one condition to be tested, the `Case` statement can be used. The above example can be rewritten as:

```
Select Case mark
    Case 75 To 100
        grade = "A"
    Case 60 To 74
        grade = "B"
    Case 50 To 59
        grade = "C"
    Case Else
        grade = "F"
End Select
```

3

Nested selection statements

If there is more than one condition to be tested, you can use a nested selection statement.

Example 3

A firm hiring new employees requires all applicants to take an aptitude test. If they pass the test, they are interviewed and if they pass the interview, they are offered employment. If they fail the interview, they are rejected. If they fail the aptitude test, they are given the opportunity to resit the test at a future date.

```
If testResult = "Pass" Then
    If interviewOK = "Pass" Then
        Console.WriteLine("Hired")
    Else
        Console.WriteLine("Rejected")
    End If
Else
    Console.WriteLine("Resit test")
End If
```

Complex Boolean expressions

Boolean expressions may include And, Or or Not.

Operator	Description
And	Returns True if both conditions are true
Or	Returns True if either or both conditions are true
Not	A True expression becomes False and vice versa

Table 3.2: Boolean operators

Example 4

Here are some complex Boolean expressions used in If statements:

(a)
```
If day = "Saturday" Or day = "Sunday" Then
    weekendRate = True
End If
```

(b)
```
If (Not day = "Saturday") And (Not day = "Sunday") Then
    weekendRate = False
Else
    weekendRate = True
End If
```

(c)
```
If (testResult = "Pass") And (interviewOK) Then
    Console.WriteLine("Hired")
Else
    Console.WriteLine("Rejected")
End If
```

Q2 In (b) above, assume `weekendRate` is initially set to `False` and `day` = "Sunday". What will `weekendRate` be set to?

Generating a random number

A random number can be generated using the `Rnd()` function. This function returns a value of data type Single between 0.0 and 1.0. Multiplying the random number will create a wider range. For example, a multiplier of 6 will create a random number between 0 and 6. To get a random integer within the range 1 to 6, use the function Math.Ceiling(number) which rounds up the number.

Note: before using the `Rnd()` function for the first time, set the random number generator using the statement `Randomize()`.

To generate a random number within a range of integers, you can declare an object, for example, `randomNumber` of type `Random`.

```
Dim randomNumber As New Random
```

To generate a random integer between a range of integers a and b you write

```
num = randomNumber.Next(a,b)
```

Note that `a` is included in the range but `b` is not.

Example 5

Generate two random numbers between 1 and 6 (inclusive) to represent the throw of two dice. If the numbers are equal, print, for example, "You threw a double 5". There are two different ways this can be programmed, using either the Rnd function or a Random object.

Using the `Rnd()` function:

```
Dim die1, die2 As Integer
Randomize()
die1 = Math.Ceiling(Rnd() * 6)
die2 = Math.Ceiling(Rnd() * 6)
If die1 = die2 Then
    Console.WriteLine("You threw a double " & die1)
End If
```

Using the `Random` object:

```
Dim RandomNumber As New Random
die1 = RandomNumber.Next(1, 7)
die2 = RandomNumber.Next(1, 7)
If die1 = die2 Then
    Console.WriteLine("You threw a double " & die1)
End If
```

Exercises

1. Write a program to allow the user to enter the length and width of a rectangle and calculate the area. If the length and width are equal, print `"This is a square of area nn.nn"`. Otherwise, print `"This is a rectangle of area nn.nn"`.

2. Write a program to display a menu of options:

   ```
   Menu
   1.Music
   2.History
   3.Design and Technology
   4.Exit
   Please enter your choice:
   ```

   The user then enters a choice and the program prints a message such as "`You chose History`". If they choose option 4, the program prints "`Goodbye`".

3. Write a program to simulate the throw of two dice and print the two numbers thrown (each between 1 and 6). Print the numbers representing the two throws.

   If the numbers on the two dice are not equal, the player's score is the sum of the numbers thrown. Print the score.

   If the numbers on the two dice are equal, the player scores twice the sum of the number thrown. Print "You threw a double", and the score.

4. Write a program to input the total value of goods purchased in a shop. A discount is subtracted from the total to find the amount owed.

   If the amount is £200 or more, 10% discount is given.

   If the amount is between £100 and £199.99, 5% discount is given.
   Print the value of goods, discount given and amount owed.

3

5. Write a program to calculate car park charges. Up to 2 hours costs £3.50, up to 4 hours £5.00, up to 12 hours £10.00. The driver enters the number of hours they require and the machine prints the current time, expiry time and charge. For example:

   ```
   Time now: 12/03/2019 17:09:54
   Expires:  12/03/2019 20:09:54
   Charge = £5.00
   ```

   Tip: Use the VB.NET data type Date. The current time can be read with the following:

   ```
   Dim currentTime As Date
   currentTime = Now()
   ```

   Hours can be added to the current time using the method AddHours():

   ```
   expiryTime = CurrentTime.AddHours(hoursRequired)
   ```

   Date data type values do not require any conversion to output. They appear as shown in the sample output above.

Chapter 4

Iteration

Objectives

- Use `For` loops (definite iteration)
- Use `While` loops (pre-condition indefinite iteration)
- Use `Repeat` loops (post-condition indefinite iteration)
- Use string functions and operators

The `For` loop

Sometimes in a program, you want to repeat a sequence of steps a certain number of times. A `For` loop can iterate over a sequence of numbers in a range in different ways. For example, the programmer can specify that a number used as a count has a range `a To b`, meaning from `a` up to `b`.

Example 1

```
'Program name: Ch 4 Example 1 For loop examples
Dim number As Integer
Dim number2 As Double

' Sample range 1: print the numbers 1 to 5
Console.WriteLine("Numbers from 1-5:")
For number = 1 To 5
    Console.Write(number & " ")
Next
Console.WriteLine()
' Sample range 2: print every third number from 1 to 16
Console.WriteLine("Every third number in range 1-16:")
```

```
For number = 1 To 16 Step 3
    Console.Write(number & " ")
Next
Console.WriteLine()

' Sample range 3: count up in halves from 1 to 5
Console.WriteLine("Counting in halves from 0 to 5:")
For number2 = 0 To 5 Step 0.5
    Console.Write(number2 & "  ")
Next
Console.WriteLine()

' Sample range 4: print every number from 5 down to 1
Console.WriteLine("Every number from 5 down to 1:")
For number = 5 To 1 Step -1
    Console.Write(number & " ")
Next
```

The output is:

```
Numbers from 1-5:
1 2 3 4 5
Every third number in range 1-16:
1 4 7 10 13 16
Counting in halves from 0 to 5:
0  0.5  1  1.5  2  2.5  3  3.5  4  4.5  5
Every number from 5 down to 1:
5 4 3 2 1
```

Note the following points in the sample ranges:

- **Sample range 1** will start with the first number specified and go up to and including the second number specified.

- **Sample range 2** shows that you can count in threes. You can increment the counter by any integer value.

- **Sample range 3** shows that you can count in halves. You can increment the counter by any integer or real value.

- **Sample range 4** shows that you can increment the counter by a negative value. The counter will then count down from the first value to the last value specified.

Nested loops

You can have one loop 'nested' inside another. The next example shows how we could print all the multiplication tables from 1 to 12.

Example 2

```
'Program name: Ch 4 Example 2 Multiplication tables
For table = 1 To 12
    Console.WriteLine(table & " Times Table ")
    For row = 1 To 12
        Console.
WriteLine(row & " x " & table & " = " & row * table)
    Next
    Console.WriteLine()
Next
```

 Q1 Write program code to do the following:

(a) Print the numbers 10 - 0 starting at 10. Then print "Lift-off!". Include a time delay of 1 second before printing each number, using the statement `Threading.Thread.Sleep(1000)`.

(b) Ask the user to enter 5 numbers. Keep a running total and print the total and average of the numbers.

The `While` loop

The `While` loop is used when the number of times the loop will be performed is initially unknown. The loop is performed as long as a specified Boolean condition is **True**. If the condition is **False** before the `While` statement is encountered, the loop will be skipped.

The Boolean condition is tested in the `While` statement at the start of the loop, and again each time the loop is completed. If it becomes **True** halfway through the loop, the remaining statements in the loop will be executed before the loop is tested.

Example 3

Write code to accept a series of integer test results from a user, find and print the maximum and minimum results. Assume all the results are between 0 and 100. The end of the input is signalled by the input of -1.

```
'Program name: Ch 4 Example 3 max and min
Dim maxResult, minResult, testResult As Integer
Console.Write("Please enter test result: ")
testResult = Console.ReadLine()
' Set maximum and minimum to first test result
maxResult = testResult
minResult = testResult
While testResult <> -1
    If testResult > maxResult Then
        maxResult = testResult
    End If
    If testResult < minResult Then
        minResult = testResult
    End If
```

4

```
        Console.Write("Please enter test result (-1 to finish): ")
        testResult = Console.ReadLine()
    End While
    Console.WriteLine()
    Console.WriteLine("Maximum test result = " & maxResult)
    Console.WriteLine("Minimum test result = " & minResult)
```

The output will be similar to this:

```
Please enter test result: 45
Please enter test result (-1 to finish): 63
Please enter test result (-1 to finish): 24
Please enter test result (-1 to finish): 33
Please enter test result (-1 to finish): 45
Please enter test result (-1 to finish): -1

Maximum test result = 63
Minimum test result = 24
```

Note carefully the technique of writing the first input statement before entering the While loop. This value is then processed and subsequent input statements are executed at the end of the loop so that as soon as −1 is input, the next thing that happens is that the condition is tested and the loop is exited.

Q2   What would be the result of setting maxResult = 0, minResult = 100, testResult = 0 at the start of the above program, and having just one ReadLine statement as the second statement in the loop?

Q3   The original program is altered so that the inputs are string values, and the condition to be tested is TestResult <> "-1". What will be output if the values 34, 19, 100, 56, -1 are input? Explain your answer.

4

Q4   Amend the program from Example 3 so that if the user enters -1 as the first input, the output will be "No results input".

The Do ... Loop **statement**

VB also provides iteration using the Do ... Loop construct. The loop is performed while a condition is True or until the condition becomes True.

Construct	Alternatives to the Example 3 loop

Do While
condition
 	
Loop
	```Do While testResult <> -1```
	`    If testResult > maxResult Then`
	`        maxResult = testResult`
	`    End If`
	`    If testResult < minResult Then`
	`        minResult = testResult`
	`    End If`
	`    Console.Write("Enter result`
	`                (-1 to finish): ")`
	`                testResult = Console.ReadLine()`
	`Loop`

Do Until
condition
 	
Loop
	```Do Until testResult = -1```
	`    If testResult > maxResult Then`
	`        maxResult = testResult`
	`    End If`
	`    If testResult < minResult Then`
	`        minResult = testResult`
	`    End If`
	`    Console.Write("Enter result`
	`                (-1 to finish): ")`
	`                testResult = Console.ReadLine()`
	`Loop`

Do
 	
Loop While
condition
	```Do```
	`    If testResult > maxResult Then`
	`        maxResult = testResult`
	`    End If`
	`    If testResult < minResult Then`
	`        minResult = testResult`
	`    End If`
	`    Console.Write("Enter result`
	`                (-1 to finish): ")`
	`                testResult = Console.ReadLine()`
	`Loop While testResult <> -1`

Do
 	
Loop Until
condition
	```Do```
	`    If testResult > maxResult Then`
	`        maxResult = testResult`
	`    End If`
	`    If testResult < minResult Then`
	`        minResult = testResult`
	`    End If`
	`    Console.Write("Enter result`
	`                (-1 to finish): ")`
	`                testResult = Console.ReadLine()`
	`Loop Until testResult = -1`

4

String processing

Loops are often used when processing strings. In the example below, the `For` loop condition is written in an alternative way known as a `For Each` loop. In this type of loop, each character in the string will be processed one by one.

Recall from Chapter 2 that the function `Len(aString)` returns the number of characters in a string.

Example 4

Count and print the number of words and the number of characters in a piece of text. You can count words by counting the number of spaces in the text and adding 1 to the total. (This assumes there is exactly one space between each word.)

```
'Program name: Ch 4 Example 4 words in sentence
Dim sentence As String
Dim numWords As Integer = 1
Console.Write("Enter a sentence: ")
sentence = Console.ReadLine()
For Each letter In sentence
    If letter = " " Then
        numWords += 1
    End If
Next
Console.WriteLine("Number of words = " & numWords)
Console.WriteLine("Number of characters = " & Len(sentence))
```

Indexing strings

Each character in a string can be referenced by its **index**, starting at 0. Thus, if a variable called `Word` contains the string `"basic"`, `Word(0)` stores `"b"`, `Word(1)` stores `"a"`, `Word(2)` stores `"s"` and so on.

Example 5

Find the number of times that the letter 'e' occurs in a sentence. This example will find both uppercase and lower case letters.

```
'Program name: Ch 4 Example 5 count Es

Dim sentence As String
Dim eTotal As Integer = 0
Console.Write("Please enter a sentence: ")
sentence = Console.ReadLine()
For Each letter In sentence
    If letter = "e" Or letter = "E" Then
        eTotal += 1
    End If
Next

Console.WriteLine("Number of 'e's in the sentence = " & eTotal)
```

4

Q5 Write a program that finds the total number of vowels (a, e, i, o, u) in a sentence. Recall from Chapter 2 that the string method `aString.ToUpper()` will return the uppercase from any lowercase letters. This will help make the condition statement shorter.

Substrings

Using indexing, you can isolate a single character in a string. Using the function `Mid()`, you can isolate anything from a single character to the whole string, so, for example, you could look at the first three characters of a car registration number, or the middle five characters of a nine-character string. Note that the Mid function indexes the characters in a string starting with 1.

Example 6

You can try out various substrings:

Program	Output

`Dim firstName, nickname, initial As String`
 	
`firstName = "Phillip"`
`nickname = Mid(firstName, 1, 5)`
`initial = Mid(firstName, 1, 1)`
`Console.WriteLine(nickname)`
`Console.WriteLine(initial)`
`Console.WriteLine(Mid(firstName, 2, 4))`
`Console.WriteLine(Mid(firstName, 1, 10))`
`Console.WriteLine(Mid(firstName, 3))`
	`Phill`
	`P`
	`hill`
	`Phillip`
	`illip`

Interrupting execution

Sometimes a logic error may result in a program looping endlessly. You can terminate (kill) a running program by selecting *Debug, Stop Debugging* from the menu bar in the IDE, or by pressing the shortcut key combination **Ctrl-C**.

Example 7

In the following example, the programmer has forgotten to write an `input` statement at the end of the `While` loop.

```
'Program name: Ch 4 Example 7 endless loop
Dim name As String
Console.Write("This program demonstrates ")
Console.WriteLine(" how you can get into an endless loop")
Console.WriteLine()
Console.WriteLine("You can stop it by selecting")
Console.WriteLine("Debug, Stop Debugging")
Console.WriteLine("from the menu in the IDE.")
Console.WriteLine()

Console.Write("Enter a name, xxx to end: ")
name = Console.ReadLine()
While name <> "xxx"
    Console.WriteLine("Number of letters
                      in name: " & Len(name))
End While
```

The output will be something like:

```
Enter a name, xxx to end: Jacob
Number of letters in name: 5
Number of letters in name: 5
Number of letters in name: 5
... (endlessly repeated)
```

Exercises

1. Write a program to generate 10 random numbers between 1 and 10, and print out the 10 numbers and the total of the numbers.

2. Extend the program in Exercise 1 to repeat the generation of 10 random numbers 1000 times. Do not print out the random numbers or the total of each set of 10 numbers – just print the average of the totals at the end of the program. Is the answer approximately what you would expect?

3. Write a program to allow the user to enter a number of 5-character product codes, beginning with the letters "AB" or "AS" followed by 3 numeric characters.

    Count and print the total number of product codes starting with "AB" and the total number of product codes ending in "00".

    Test your program by entering product codes AS123, AS101, AB111, AB345, CD222, AB200.

4

Chapter 5

Arrays and tuples

Objectives

- Understand why arrays are useful

- Declare an array and use array methods

- Use one- and two-dimensional arrays to solve problems

- Distinguish between arrays and tuples

Arrays

An array is a type of sequence, like a string. However, unlike a string, which can contain only characters, an array can contain elements of any data type as long as each element in the array is of the same type. An array could contain, for example, several names:

```
Dim name = {"Mark", "Juan", "Ali", "Cathy", "Sylvia", "Noah"}
```

These names can be indexed, just like the elements of a string, so `name(0)` stores "Mark" and `name(5)` stores "Noah".

Example 1

Write code to print the names in an array called `name` on separate lines

```
Dim name = {"Mark", "Juan", "Ali", "Cathy", "Sylvia", "Noah"}
For index = 0 To name.Length() - 1
    Console.WriteLine(name(index))
Next
```

> **Q1**
>
> What will happen if you write
> ```
> Dim name = {"Mark", "Juan", "Ali", "Cathy",
> "Sylvia", "Noah"}
> For index = 0 To 6
>     Console.WriteLine(name(index))
> Next
> ```

Operations on arrays

Some array methods are shown in the table below. Assume `a = {45,13,19,13,8}`.

Array operation	Description	Example	array contents	Return value
Count()	Counts the elements in the array	`a.Count()`	{45, 13, 19, 13, 8}	5
Length()	Return the number of elements	`a.Length()`	{45, 13, 19, 13, 8}	5
Contains(Item)	Returns True if Item exists in array, False otherwise	`a.Contains (13)`	{45, 13, 19, 13, 8}	True
Max()	Returns the largest value	`a.Max()`	{45, 13, 19, 13, 8}	45
Min()	Returns the smallest value	`a.Min()`	{45, 13, 19, 13, 8}	8
Sum()	Returns the sum of all elements of a numeric array	`a.Sum()`	{45, 13, 19, 13, 8}	98
Average()	Returns the average of all elements of a numeric array	`a.Average()`	{45, 13, 19, 13, 8}	19.6

Table 5.1 Array operations

Example 2

Determine whether the number `100` is in the array
`numbers = {56,78,100,45,88,71}`, and if so, print its index.

```
'Program name: Ch 5 Example 2 Array of numbers
Dim numbers = {56, 78, 100, 45, 88, 71}
Dim index = Array.IndexOf(numbers, 100)

If index = -1 Then
    Console.WriteLine("100 is not in the array")
Else
    Console.WriteLine("100 is at index number: " & index)
End If
```

An array is a static data structure, that means it is fixed in size. The elements of an array must all be of the same data type.

5

Initialising an array

Example 2 shows one way in which the array `numbers` can be initialised with an array of **literals** which are inside braces ({ }). An alternative to this is:

```
Dim numbers(5) As Integer
For index = 0 To 5
    numbers(index) = 10
Next
```

This program first creates an array with 6 elements (from index 0 to index 5). When an array is created, it will first be initialised with 0 in each element. The For loop shows how the array can then be initialised with the number 10 in each element.

Array processing

Items are often held in arrays for further processing. The items may be input by the user or read from a file on disk, for example. Sometimes the array values may be defined in the program.

Example 3

Define an array containing the names of students in a class. Ask the user to input the exam results for each student. Print a report showing the data with column headings

```
Student                 Exam mark
```

At the end of the report, print the name of the student with the highest mark, and the mark obtained.

```
'Program name: Ch 5 Example 3 Exam results
'program prints list of exam results and the highest result.
Dim studentNames = {"Afridi", "Angela", "Justin", "Nicola"}
Dim topStudent As String = ""
Dim topMark = 0
Dim numberOfStudents = studentNames.Length()
Dim results(numberOfStudents)
For student = 0 To numberOfStudents - 1
    Console.Write("Enter mark for "
                    & studentNames(student) & ": ")
    Dim mark As Integer = Console.ReadLine()
    results(student) = mark
    If mark > topMark Then
        topMark = mark
        topStudent = studentNames(student)
    End If
Next
Console.WriteLine("Student" & vbTab & "Exam mark")
For student = 0 To numberOfStudents - 1
    Console.WriteLine(studentNames(student)
                    & vbTab & results(student))
Next
Console.WriteLine("Top result: " & topStudent & " " & topMark)
Console.ReadLine()
```

This produces output in the format:

```
Enter mark for Afridi: 56
Enter mark for Angela: 67
Enter mark for Justin: 71
Enter mark for Nicola: 52
Student Exam mark
Afridi  56
Angela  67
Justin  71
Nicola  52
Top result: Justin 71
```

Two-dimensional arrays

In some applications, you may need a table of values rather than a one-dimensional array. Suppose you wanted to hold the data in the following table, which shows the average maximum and minimum temperatures (°C) in London for each month of the year.

Month	Max temp (°C)	Min temp (°C)
January	6	3
February	7	3
March	10	4
April	13	6
May	17	9
June	20	12
July	22	14
August	21	14
September	19	12
October	14	9
November	10	6
December	7	3

The numeric values could be stored in a two-dimensional array named MonthlyAvg:

```
Dim monthlyAvg = {{6, 3},
                  {7, 3},
                  {10, 4},
```

and so on down to:

```
                  {7, 3}}
```

Each element of the two-dimensional array is referred to by two indices giving the row index (between 0 and 11) and column index (between 0 and 1).

The average maximum temperature in March would be referred to as `MonthlyAvg(2,0)`.

`monthlyAvg.length()` will return 24 as there are 24 items in the 2D-array.
`monthlyAvg.getLength(0)` will return the number of rows (12) in the 2D-array.

Q2 How would you refer to the average minimum temperature for November?

Q3 Write a statement to print the data for December, giving the month and the two temperatures in the format `[monthname, maxtemp, mintemp]`

Q4 What will be printed by the statement below?
```
Console.WriteLine(monthlyAvg.getLength(1))
```

Example 4

Write a program to enable a user to enter the average maximum and minimum temperatures for each month and store them in a two-dimensional array named `monthlyAvg`. Print the monthly data when it has all been entered.

Some things to note about this program:

- The month names are supplied in a one-dimensional string array so that the user does not have to enter them.

- The table `monthlyAvg` which will hold the monthly averages is declared as an integer array of 12 rows and 2 columns.

- Rows and columns are numbered from 0, so "December" is in row 11.

```
'Program name: Ch 5 Example 4 2-D list of temperatures
'program to allow the user to enter monthly average maximum
'and minimum temperatures
Dim monthName = {"January", "February", "March", "April",
                 "May", "June", "July", "August",
                 "September", "October",
                 "November", "December"}
Dim monthlyAvg(11, 1) As Integer
```

```
For m = 0 To 11
    Console.WriteLine("Enter average maximum and
                      minimum for " & monthName(m))
    Console.Write("Maximum: ")
    monthlyAvg(m, 0) = Console.ReadLine()
    Console.Write("Minimum: ")
    monthlyAvg(m, 1) = Console.ReadLine()
Next
' now print the list
Console.WriteLine()
For m = 0 To 11
    Console.WriteLine(monthName(m) & vbTab &
                     monthlyAvg(m, 0) & vbTab&
                     monthlyAvg(m, 1))
Next
```

Tuples

Tuples are very similar to arrays, with one major difference: they can store data items of different data types. Like an array, a tuple can hold a number of items that can be indexed. In VB.NET tuples are **mutable**, this means the values can be changed. The following example demonstrates this.

A tuple is written in parentheses (round brackets) rather than braces {}.

Example 5

```
'Program Name: Ch 5 Example 5 Tuples
Dim student = ("Fred", 2003, False)
Console.WriteLine(student)
student.Item3 = True
Console.WriteLine("Name: " & student.Item1)
Console.WriteLine("Year of birth: " & student.Item2)
Console.WriteLine("Full-time student? " & student.Item3)
Console.Write("Press Enter to exit")
Console.ReadLine()
```

Produces the output

```
(Fred, 2003, False)
Name: Fred
Year of birth: 2003
Full-time student? True
Press Enter to exit
```

5

Arrays of tuples

When you want to store rows of data items that are of different data types, you can use an array of tuples.

Example 6

```
'Program Name: Ch 5 Example 6 Arrays of tuples
Dim studentMarks = {("Harvey", "Ron", 56),
                    ("Jones", "Alan", 85),
                    ("Lansbury", "Christine", 68),
                    ("Mills", "David", 72)}
For row = 0 To studentMarks.GetLength(0) - 1
    Console.WriteLine(studentMarks(row).Item1)
Next
```

Produces the output:

```
Harvey
Jones
Lansbury
Mills
```

Structures

You can use a structure type to combine items of different data types.

To use a structure, first declare the data items (fields) you intend to store in the structure:

```
Structure StudentRecord
    Dim firstName As String
    Dim yearOfBirth As Integer
    Dim isFullTimeStudent As Boolean
End Structure
```

Then declare a variable of that structure type:

```
Dim student As StudentRecord
```

You access the individual fields using the dot notation:

```
Dim student As StudentRecord
student.FirstName = "Fred"
Student.YearOfBirth = 2003
Student.IsFullTimeStudent = True
```

Arrays of structures

You can store records of the same type in an array.

Example 7

Write a program to store student records. Each student record will contain the first name, year of birth and whether the student is a full-time student. There will be five students stored.

```
'Program Name: Ch 5 Example 7 Arrays of structures
Module Module1
    Structure StudentRecord
        Dim firstName As String
        Dim yearOfBirth As Integer
        Dim isFullTimeStudent As Boolean
    End Structure

    Sub Main()
        Dim student(5) As StudentRecord

        For index = 0 To student.Length - 1
            Console.Write("Enter first name: ")
            student(index).firstName = Console.ReadLine()
            Console.Write("Enter year of birth: ")
            student(index).yearOfBirth = Console.ReadLine()
            student(index).isFullTimeStudent = True
        Next
        For index = 0 To student.Length - 1
            Console.WriteLine(student(index).firstName)
        Next
        Console.Write("Press Enter to exit ")
        Console.ReadLine()
    End Sub
End Module
```

Exercises

1. Write statements to:

   (a) define a string array called fruit for 5 elements

   (b) assign string element "apple" to the first array element

   (c) define an array named scores containing 20 elements, each storing 10.

2. Write a program to accept a student name, and the marks obtained on 10 weekly tests. Print the name, average mark, top mark and the bottom mark. (Use Max(), Min() and Average())

3. Extend the program shown in Example 3 to find the months with the hottest average temperature and the coldest average temperature. Print the month names and relevant temperatures of these months.

4. Write a program to simulate how the top scores of several players playing an online game many times could be held in an array.

   (a) Define a two-dimensional array which will hold in the same row, a user ID and their top score for an online game. The arrays are to be initialised with the following values:

   ```
   UserID  TopScore
   AAA01   135
   BBB01    87
   CCC01   188
   DDD01   109
   ```

   (b) Ask a user to enter their ID. Check if the user ID is in the list. If it is then output 'User account exists'.

   (c) Generate a random number between 50 and 100 to represent the score for this game. Locate the user. Check whether the new score is greater than the score in the array and if so, replace it.

   (d) Print the user IDs and scores.

   Repeat steps **b** to **d** until a UserID of xxx is entered.

   Note: *Alternatively you can declare an array of structures to store the data in a one-dimensional array.*

5

Chapter 6
Validating user input

Objectives

- Be able to validate user input
- Use exception handling routines
- Use regular expressions to validate input data

Validating user input

Whatever a user is asked to enter, if there is any possibility that the input could cause the program to crash or give a wrong result, it should be validated.

There are different types of validation check that can be carried out, for example:

Length check, **type check** and **format check**.

Length check

If data such as a product code input by the user should be a certain length, for example, 6 characters, you can check this using the `Len()` function and ask the user to re-input the data if it is invalid, until they get it right.

```
Dim prodCode = ""
While Len(prodCode) <> 6
    Console.Write("Please enter 6-character product code: ")
    prodCode = Console.ReadLine()
    If Len(prodCode) <> 6 Then
        Console.WriteLine("Invalid code")
    End If
End While
```

Q1 Rewrite this validation routine to check if the product code is between 6 and 10 characters long.

Type check

If the user input is assigned to an integer or real number and the user has not entered number characters, the program will crash unless steps are taken to prevent this.

One method of checking that a valid number has been entered is to use the `Try...Catch...End Try` clause. This will catch an error and prevent crashing.

Example 1

Write a program to calculate the total and average of several numbers entered by the user. The end of the input is to be signalled by the user entering "end".

```
'Program name: Ch 6 Example 1 try catch
Console.WriteLine("This program accepts integers or real
          numbers " & "and finds their total and average.")
Console.WriteLine("Enter 'end' to signal end of data entry.")
Dim total = 0
Dim count = 0
Dim numberString As String
Dim number, average As Double
Console.Write("Please enter a number: ")
numberString = Console.ReadLine()
While numberString.ToLower() <> "end"
    Try
        number = CDbl(numberString) ' convert String to Double
        total += number
        count += 1
    Catch
        'ValueError
        Console.WriteLine("This is not a number")
    End Try
    Console.Write("Enter next number, 'end' to finish : ")
    numberString = Console.ReadLine()
End While
average = total / count
Console.WriteLine()
Console.WriteLine("Total = " & total & " Average = "
                & Math.Round(average, 2))
```

The ASCII code

The standard ASCII code uses 7 bits to represent 128 different combinations of binary digits, more than enough to represent all the characters on a standard English language keyboard. The table of ASCII characters and the equivalent decimal and binary characters is shown on the next page. The first 32 characters represent non-printing characters such as *Backspace*, *Enter* and *Escape* and are not shown in the table.

ASCII	DEC	Binary	ASCII	DEC	Binary	ASCII	DEC	Binary
space	032	010 0000	@	064	100 0000	`	096	110 0000
!	033	010 0001	A	065	100 0001	a	097	110 0001
"	034	010 0010	B	066	100 0010	b	098	110 0010
#	035	010 0011	C	067	100 0011	c	099	110 0011
$	036	010 0100	D	068	100 0100	d	100	110 0100
%	037	010 0101	E	069	100 0101	e	101	110 0101
&	038	010 0110	F	070	100 0110	f	102	110 0110
'	039	010 0111	G	071	100 0111	g	103	110 0111
(	040	010 1000	H	072	100 1000	h	104	110 1000
)	041	010 1001	I	073	100 1001	i	105	110 1001
*	042	010 1010	J	074	100 1010	j	106	110 1010
+	043	010 1011	K	075	100 1011	k	107	110 1011
,	044	010 1100	L	076	100 1100	l	108	110 1100
-	045	010 1101	M	077	100 1101	m	109	110 1101
.	046	010 1110	N	078	100 1110	n	110	110 1110
/	047	010 1111	O	079	100 1111	o	111	110 1111
0	048	011 0000	P	080	101 0000	p	112	111 0000
1	049	011 0001	Q	081	101 0001	q	113	111 0001
2	050	011 0010	R	082	101 0010	r	114	111 0010
3	051	011 0011	S	083	101 0011	s	115	111 0011
4	052	011 0100	T	084	101 0100	t	116	111 0100
5	053	011 0101	U	085	101 0101	u	117	111 0101
6	054	011 0110	V	086	101 0110	v	118	111 0110
7	055	011 0111	W	087	101 0111	w	119	111 0111
8	056	011 1000	X	088	101 1000	x	120	111 1000
9	057	011 1001	Y	089	101 1001	y	121	111 1001
:	058	011 1010	Z	090	101 1010	z	122	111 1010
;	059	011 1011	[	091	101 1011	{	123	111 1011
<	060	011 1100	\	092	101 1100	|	124	111 1100
=	061	011 1101	]	093	101 1101	}	125	111 1101
>	062	011 1110	^	094	101 1110	~	126	111 1110
?	063	011 1111	_	095	101 1111	DEL	127	111 1111

Table 6.1: ASCII character table

6

Functions Asc() and Chr()

These two functions convert between a character and its ASCII value. For example:

```
Console.WriteLine(Chr(106))
Console.WriteLine(Asc("s"))
```

They will output:

```
j
115
```

Example 2

Ask the user to enter a new password. The password must contain at least one uppercase letter. If it does not, the user is asked to input another password.

One way of checking that a character is an uppercase letter is to convert it to ASCII and check that its decimal equivalent is between 65 and 90.

```
'Program name: Ch 6 Example 2 validate password
Console.WriteLine("Password must contain at least one
                   uppercase letter")
Dim password As String
Dim passwordValid = False
Console.Write("Please enter new password: ")
password = Console.ReadLine()
While Not passwordValid
    For index = 0 To Len(password) - 1
        If Asc(password(index)) >= 65 And Asc(password(index))
           <= 90 Then
              passwordValid = True
        End If
    Next
    If Not passwordValid Then
        Console.Write("Invalid - please enter new password: ")
        password = Console.ReadLine()
    End If
End While
Console.WriteLine("Password accepted")
```

Example 3

Once the user has set a password for a particular application, they will be asked to enter it when they log on, and it will be compared with a stored password. They are typically given three attempts to get it right.

The following program shows one method of doing this. The Boolean variable PasswordValid acts as a **flag**, which if False indicates an invalid password.

```
'Program name: Ch 6 Example 3 compare password
'Program to check a user's password
Dim storedPassword = "Secret246"
Dim password As String
Dim passwordValid = False
Dim attempt = 1
While attempt <= 3 And Not passwordValid
    Console.Write("Input password: ")
    password = Console.ReadLine()
    If password = storedPassword Then
        passwordValid = True
    Else
        Console.WriteLine("This password is not correct ... ")
        attempt += 1
    End If
End While
If PasswordValid Then
    Console.WriteLine("Password accepted")
Else
    Console.WriteLine("Log on unsuccessful")
End If
```

Regular expressions

A regular expression is a special sequence of characters that can be used to check for valid user input. The module `RegularExpressions` provides support for regular expressions and needs to be imported at the start of the program.

A list of some of the most common regular expressions is given below.

Expression	Description
[A-R]	Uppercase letter from A to R
[ADF]	Matches A, D or F
[A-Z]{3}	Exactly three uppercase letters from A to Z
[A-Z]{1,2}	One or two uppercase letters from A to Z
[0-9]{3,}	Three or more digits
[0-5]	Digit between 0 and 5
\d	Digit
[a-z]+	One or more lowercase characters
[a-z]*	Zero or more lowercase characters
[a-z]?	0 or 1 lowercase characters
\s	space (e.g. [A-Z]\s\d{1,2} will find B 56 and B 1 valid, B52 and BN 3 invalid
A|B	A or B

Table 6.2: Regular expressions

6

Note that instead of writing \s to indicate a space in a regular expression, you can simply leave a space.

These expressions may be combined to perform a format check or match complex combinations of letters and numbers, for example, different postcodes or car registration numbers. Imports System.Text.RegularExpressions must be used at the start of the program in order to use regular expressions.

Example 4

Use a regular expression to check that a userID entered by the user consists of one or two uppercase letters followed by three digits.

```
Imports System.Text.RegularExpressions

Module Module1
    Sub Main()
        'Program name: Ch6 Example 4 regular expression1
        Dim re As Regex = New Regex("[A-Z]{1,2}[0-9]{3}")
        Dim userID As String
        Dim validID = False
        Console.Write("Enter your user ID: ")
        userID = Console.ReadLine()
        validID = Re.IsMatch(UserID)
        If validID Then
            Console.WriteLine("Valid ID entered")
        Else
            Console.WriteLine("Invalid ID")
        End If

        Console.WriteLine("Press Enter to exit ")
        Console.ReadLine()
    End Sub
End Module
```

Example 5

A product code starts with one or two uppercase letters, followed by four or more digits, and ends with either H or G. Accept a product code from the user and use a regular expression to validate it.

```
Imports System.Text.RegularExpressions

Module Module1
    Sub Main()
        'Program name: Ch6 Example 5 regular expression2
        'program uses a regular expression to check for
        valid product code
        Dim re As Regex = New Regex("[A-Z]{1,2}[0-9]
                                     {4,[H,G]")
        Dim productCode As String = ""
        Dim valid = False
```

```
            While productCode <> "x"
                Console.Write("Enter a product code ('x' to end): ")
                productCode = Console.ReadLine()
                valid = re.IsMatch(productCode)
                If valid Then
                    Console.WriteLine("Valid
                    product code entered")
                Else
                    Console.WriteLine("Invalid product code")
                End If
            End While
            Console.WriteLine("Press Enter to exit ")
            Console.ReadLine()
        End Sub
End Module
```

Example 6

Use a regular expression to check that a password contains at least one digit.

```
    Imports System.Text.RegularExpressions

    Module Module1
        Sub Main()
            'Program name: Ch6 Example 6 regular expression3
            'program to check for at least one digit in a password
            Dim re As Regex = New Regex("[a-zA-Z]*\d[a-zA-Z0-9]*")
            Dim password As String
            Dim validPassword = False
            Console.Write("Enter password: ")
            password = Console.ReadLine()
            validPassword = re.IsMatch(password)
            If validPassword Then
                Console.WriteLine("Valid password")
            Else
                Console.WriteLine("Invalid password")
            End If
            Console.WriteLine("Press Enter to exit ")
            Console.ReadLine()
        End Sub
    End Module
```

6

Exercises

1. A drama group wants to record the number of tickets sold for each of their four performances. Ask the user to enter the number of tickets sold for each performance. The number must be between 0 and 120. Print an error message if an invalid number is entered, and ask them to re-enter until they enter a valid number. Print the total number of tickets sold and the average attendance for a performance.

2. Write a program to ask the user to enter a car registration number, which must be in the format AANN AAA. Validate the entry and if invalid, ask the user to re-enter it.

3. Write a program to ask a user to enter their email address. They should then be asked to enter it again, and if it does not match the first entry, the user is asked to start over. Print a suitable message when the email address is correctly verified.

4. Write a program to ask a user to enter a new password. The password must be between 8 and 15 characters long and have at least one lowercase letter, one uppercase letter and one numeric character. If it does not, the user should repeatedly be asked to enter a different password until they enter a valid one.

5. Passwords on a file are to be stored in encrypted form so that they cannot easily be hacked by someone looking at the file.

   A simple 'Caesar cipher' is used to encrypt a password by adding 3 to the ASCII value of each letter, converting this back to a character and storing the result. For example, the password BENXY3 would be stored as EHQAB6.

   Write a program to ask a user to enter a password. This is then encrypted and checked against the encrypted password held in the variable `storedPassword`. Assume, for test purposes, that the value held in `storedPassword` is EHQAB6.

   If the user enters an incorrect password, they are given two more attempts to get it right before being denied access.

6

Chapter 7
Searching and sorting

Objectives

- Use the dictionary data structure to look up data

- Sort a one-dimensional list in ascending or descending sequence

Dictionary data structure

You have used **strings**, **arrays** and **tuples** in Chapters 4 and 5. These are all known as **collection** data types because they can consist of several items of data. There is another useful collection data type called a **dictionary**.

A dictionary stores data items in pairs, with each pair consisting of a **key** and a **value**. It functions just like a printed dictionary, where you can look up a word (the key) and find its definition (the value).

Like an array, a dictionary is **mutable**, meaning that its values can be changed.

A dictionary is written in curly brackets, with each key-value pair being enclosed in curly brackets separated by commas. In the statements shown below, the dictionary is called `StudentMarks` and contains a number of student names and the mark they obtained in a test.

```
Dim studentMarks As New Dictionary(Of String, Integer) From
    {{"Wesley", 5}, {"Jo", 9}, {"Betty", 6}, {"Robina", 5}}
For Each key In studentMarks.Keys
    Console.WriteLine("Key:  " & key & vbTab & "Value: " &
    studentMarks.Item(key))
Next
```

produces the output:

```
Key:   Wesley       Value: 5
Key:   Jo           Value: 9
Key:   Betty        Value: 6
Key:   Robina       Value: 5
```

To look up the mark obtained by a particular student (the key), write the name of the dictionary followed by the key in brackets. You cannot index a dictionary in the same way as an array, using an index number – an item can only be accessed through its key.

The statement

```
Console.WriteLine("Betty: " & studentMarks("Betty"))
```

produces the output:

```
Betty: 6
```

Q1 Write a statement to print the mark obtained by Robina.

The table below shows some of the most useful built-in dictionary methods.

Method	Description
ContainsKey(key)	Finds if a key is present in the dictionary
Add(key, value)	Adds a key to the dictionary
Keys	Returns all the keys in the dictionary
Remove(key)	Removes an item from the dictionary

Table 7.1: Useful dictionary methods

Example 1a: Looking up a value

If you try to print the mark for a student whose name is not in the dictionary, it will return an error. To avoid this, you should test whether the key is in the dictionary before trying to access it.

```
Dim studentMarks As New Dictionary(Of String, Integer) From
    {{"Wesley", 5}, {"Jo", 9}, {"Betty", 6}, {"Robina", 5}}
Dim name As String
Console.Write("Enter a student name to look up: ")
name = Console.ReadLine()
If studentMarks.ContainsKey(name) Then
    Console.WriteLine("Mark: " & studentMarks(name))
Else
    Console.WriteLine("Name not found")
End If
```

Example 1b: Adding a new key-value pair

Before adding a new key-value pair, you should check that the key is not already in the dictionary:

```
Console.Write("Enter a student name to add: ")
name = Console.ReadLine()
If studentMarks.ContainsKey(name) Then
    Console.WriteLine("Name is already in the marks record")
Else
    Console.Write("Enter mark: ")
    Dim mark = Console.ReadLine()
    studentMarks(name) = mark  ' alternative:
    studentMarks.Add(name, mark)
End If
```

Example 1c: Editing a value in an existing key,value pair

```
Console.Write("Enter a student name to edit their mark: ")
name = Console.ReadLine()
If studentMarks.ContainsKey(name) Then
    Console.Write("Enter mark: ")
    Dim mark = Console.ReadLine()
    studentMarks(name) = mark
Else
    Console.WriteLine("Name not found")
End If
```

Example 1d: Deleting a key:value pair

```
Console.Write("Enter a student name to delete: ")
name = Console.ReadLine()
If studentMarks.ContainsKey(name) Then
    studentMarks.Remove(name)
Else
    Console.WriteLine("Name not found")
End If
```

7

Example 1e: Sorting a dictionary in order of keys

VB has a collection data type `SortedDictionary`. This works like a dictionary but with the entries sorted by key value.

```
Dim studentsSorted As New SortedDictionary(Of String,
                Integer) From {{"Wesley", 5}, {"Jo", 9},
                {"Betty", 6}, {"Robina", 5}}
Console.WriteLine("Sorted names and marks")
For Each name In studentsSorted.Keys
    Console.WriteLine(name & vbTab & studentsSorted(name))
Next
```

Produces the output:

```
Sorted names and marks
Betty    6
Jo       9
Robina   5
Wesley   5
```

The dictionary data structure is most useful for looking things up. For many other applications, a **list** is more flexible.

Adding to a list

To add a value to a list, the `Add()` method can be used.

```
Dim aList As New List(Of Integer) From {6, 2, 8, 4, 0, 2, 33}
aList.Add(12)
```

Sorting a list

To sort a list, the `Sort()` method can be used. To sort a list in reverse order use the `Reverse()` method.

Example 2

```
Dim aList As New List(Of Integer) From {6, 2, 8, 4, 0, 2, 33}
For Each item In aList
    Console.Write(item & " ")
Next
Console.WriteLine()
aList.Sort()
Console.WriteLine("Sorted list: ")
For Each item In aList
    Console.Write(item & " ")
Next
aList.Reverse()
Console.WriteLine("...and in reverse order:")
For Each item In aList
    Console.Write(item & " ")
Next
```

Produces the output:

```
6 2 8 4 0 2 33
Sorted list:
0 2 2 4 6 8 33 ...and in reverse order:
33 8 6 4 2 2 0
```

Storing a list in a dictionary

The value in the `key:value` pairs of a dictionary can itself be a list. For example, suppose you wanted to store a dictionary of anagrams, for example:

angel: angle, glean

trade: rated, tread

predator: parroted, teardrop

garden: danger, gander, ranged

The dictionary could be generated like this:

```
Dim anagrams As New Dictionary(Of String, List(Of String))
anagrams.Add("angel", New List(Of String) From {"angle",
        "glean"})
anagrams.Add("trade", New List(Of String) From {"rated",
        "tread"})
anagrams.Add("predator", New List(Of String) From {"parroted",
        "teardrop"})
anagrams.Add("garden", New List(Of String) From {"danger",
        "gander", "ranged"})
anagrams.Add("berate", New List(Of String) From {"beater",
        "rebate"})
```

7

Exercises

1. Write a program in which a dictionary of anagrams is pre-defined. The program asks the user to enter a word and then returns a list of all the anagrams of that word, or "Word not found" if the word is not in the dictionary. The user can continue to enter words until they enter "end" to quit.

2. Write a program which stores a dictionary of names and 2-digit telephone extensions. Display a menu of options from which the user can choose:

   1. Look up a telephone number

   2. Add a new name and telephone number

   3. Edit a telephone number

   4. Delete an entry

   5. Print phone directory in name sequence

   6. Quit

   Implement each of these choices.

3. Declare a structure TemperatureRecord to store the month name and the minimum and maximum temperatures for the month.

   Store the following data in an array of TemperatureRecord. Print the data.

Month	Max temp (°C)	Min temp (°C)
January	6	3
February	7	3
March	10	4
April	13	6
May	17	9
June	20	12
July	22	14
August	21	14
September	19	12
October	14	9
November	10	6
December	7	3

Table 1

4. Edit the program from Exercise 3 to output a list of all months in which the minimum temperature is below 9°C. Show the month name, maximum and minimum. Also, output a list of months with a maximum temperature of 20°C or above.

7

Chapter 8

Procedures and functions

Objectives

- Write subroutines with and without parameters
- Pass values to subroutines through parameters
- Accept return values from functions and procedures
- Understand and use local and global variables
- Divide a program up into separate subroutines

Types of subroutine

A **subroutine** is a self-contained section of code that performs one specific task. As your programs become larger, using subroutines allows you to break up the program into smaller chunks that are easier to understand, debug and maintain.

Visual Basic provides two types of subroutine: **functions** and **procedures**.

- A **procedure** is a subroutine which performs a specific task, such as for example displaying the rules of a game. It is called simply by writing the name of the procedure with any parameters if necessary in parentheses. The first line is, for example:

```
Sub DisplayRules()
```

The procedure is called by simply writing its name:

```
DisplayRules()
```

- A **function** always returns one value. As with a procedure, it can have zero, one or more parameters. A `Return` statement is used to return the calculated value to the main program. The first line is, for example:

```
Function Total(a, b, c) As Single
```

The function is usually called using an assignment statement or as part of an expression:

```
sum = Total(a, b, c)
result = Total(a, b, c) + 5
```

Built-in subroutines

You have already used some **built-in functions** such as `Asc()`, `Chr()`, `Len()` and `Mid()`. These functions are part of the Visual Basic language.

The examples below show that there are different ways of calling a function. For example, the function `Asc()` returns the ASCII value of a character. For instance:

```
asciiValue = Asc("f")
    Console.WriteLine(asciiValue)
```

In the above example, the first statement calls the function `Asc()`, passing it a **parameter** `"f"`, and assigns the value calculated by the function to a variable called `asciiValue`.

In the next example, the function `Asc()` is called without explicitly assigning it to a variable, passing it the parameter `"a"`.

```
Dim newValue As Integer
Dim newChar As Char
newValue = Asc("a") + 3
newChar = Chr(newValue)
Console.WriteLine(newChar)
```

This will output:

```
d
```

Notice that `Console.WriteLine()` is a procedure. It is called by simply writing the name of the procedure with one or more parameters in parentheses. It doesn't return a value.

`Console.ReadLine()`, by contrast, is a function. It returns a value which can then be assigned to a variable.

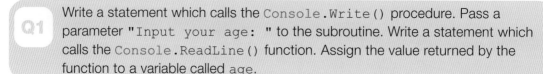

Q1 Write a statement which calls the `Console.Write()` procedure. Pass a parameter `"Input your age: "` to the subroutine. Write a statement which calls the `Console.ReadLine()` function. Assign the value returned by the function to a variable called `age`.

Writing your own functions

- A programmer-written function starts with the keyword `Function` followed by the function name and any parameters in brackets.

- The data type of the return value is then given.

- All the statements within the function are automatically indented.

- The function ends with the line `End Function`.

Writing your own procedures

- A programmer-written procedure starts with the keyword `Sub` (for subroutine) followed by any parameters in brackets.

- All the statements within the procedure are automatically indented.

- The procedure ends with the line `End Sub`.

- Both procedures (subroutines) and functions are called by writing their name. In the same way, you call an inbuilt function such as `Asc()` or `Chr()`.

Example 1

Write a subroutine (procedure) which asks the user for their name and then prints `"Hello, Jo"` or whatever name the user enters.

```
'Program name: Ch 8 Example 1 print a greeting v1
'program to get name and print a greeting

Sub GetAndPrintName()
    'This function asks the user to enter their name,
    'and then prints a greeting
    Dim name As String
    Console.Write("Please enter your name: ")
    name = Console.ReadLine()
    Console.WriteLine("Hello " & name)
End Sub

Sub Main()
    GetAndPrintName()
    Console.ReadLine()
End Sub
```

The line

```
GetAndPrintName()
```

is the **call** statement that tells the program to go and execute the procedure. The subroutine may be called many times within the program.

Using parameters and return values

Just as with built-in functions, you can provide parameters for the subroutine to use, and if it is a function, receive values back. The subroutine in Example 1 would probably be more useful if it could be used to print different messages and return the name entered by the user. This would allow it to be used in other circumstances or applications.

Example 2

In this example, the subroutine (function) prints a message specified as a parameter in the statement which calls the subroutine. The name entered by the user is passed back to the variable called `PlayerName`, using a `Return` statement.

```
'Program name: Ch 8 Example 2 print a greeting v2
'program to get name and print a greeting

Function GetAndPrintName(message) As String
    'This function asks the user to enter their name,
    'and then prints a greeting
    Dim name As String
    Console.Write("Please enter your name: ")
    name = Console.ReadLine()
    Console.WriteLine(message & " " & name)
    Return name
End Function

Sub Main()
    Dim playerName As String
    playerName = GetAndPrintName("Hello")
    Console.WriteLine(playerName & " is Player 1")
    Console.ReadLine()
End Sub
```

8

Q2 What will be output by the above program?

Q3 Write a subroutine called `Birthday()` which accepts as parameters a name and age, and prints out, for example:

Happy Birthday, Amy! You're 3 today!

Using an XML documentation block

You can document your program with an XML documentation block. This is used in Example 3 below. It can spread over as many lines as you like, enclosed in the XML tags <summary> and </summary> at the head of a program.

Example 3

Write a subroutine named `DisplayRules()` to display the rules of a game. Write a statement to call the subroutine.

```
Module Module1
    '''<summary>
    '''Program name: Ch 8 Example 3 using a docstring
    '''Author: PG Online
    '''Date written: 01/07/2019
    '''</summary>
    '''<summary>DisplayRules will display the game rules
    '''</summary>
    Sub DisplayRules()
        Console.WriteLine("
        The rules of the game are as follows:
        Players take turns to throw two dice.
        If the throw is a 'double', etc.
        ")
    End Sub

    Sub Main()
        DisplayRules()
        Console.Write("Press Enter to exit")
        Console.ReadLine()
    End Sub
End Module
```

In this example, there is no need to pass any parameters because the rules will always be the same. Nothing is returned from the subroutine so there is no `return` statement.

Example 4

Here is an example of a program which uses a function to find the average of three numbers.

```
Module Module1
    'Program name: Ch 8 Example 4 find average v1
    Function FindAverage(x As Double, y As Double, z As
    Double) As Double
        Dim total, average As Double
        total = x + y + z
        average = total / 3
        Return average
    End Function

    Sub main()
        Dim num1, num2, num3, result As Double
        Console.WriteLine("This program uses a function
                          to find the average of 3 numbers")
        Console.Write("Enter first number: ")
        num1 = Console.ReadLine()
        Console.Write("Enter second number: ")
```

```
        num2 = Console.ReadLine()
        Console.Write("Enter third number: ")
        num3 = Console.ReadLine()
        result = FindAverage(num1, num2, num3)
        Console.WriteLine("Average is " & result)

        Console.ReadLine()
    End Sub
End Module
```

The parameters `num1`, `num2` and `num3` will be referred to as `x`, `y` and `z` in the function. The order in which you write the parameters in the statement which calls the function should be the same as the order in which they appear in the function heading.

Returning several values from a subroutine

A function returns one value. To return more than one value, they can be stored in an array and then the array can be returned by the function. This is demonstrated in Example 5 below.

Example 5

The program that was given in Example 4 could be further split up so that each part of it is performed by a subroutine, and the main program is just a series of subroutine calls. Of course, you would be unlikely to do this with such a trivial program, but the example below illustrates several points.

```
Module Module1
    'Program name: Ch 8 Example 5 find average v2
    Function FindAverage(numbers As Array) As Double
        Dim total = 0
        For i = 0 To numbers.Length - 1
            total += numbers(i)
        Next
        Dim average = total / numbers.Length
        Return average
    End Function
    Sub PrintHeading()
        Console.WriteLine("This program uses a function
                          to find the average of 3 numbers")
    End Sub

    Function UserInput()
        Console.Write("Enter first number: ")
        Dim x = Console.ReadLine()
        Console.Write("Enter second number: ")
        Dim y = Console.ReadLine()
        Console.Write("Enter third number: ")
        Dim z = Console.ReadLine()
        Return {x, y, z}
    End Function
```

8

```
      Sub  PrintResult(answer)
          Console.WriteLine("Average is " & answer)
      End  Sub

      Sub  Main()
          PrintHeading()
          Dim  numbers = UserInput()
          Dim  average = FindAverage(numbers)
          PrintResult(average)

          Console.ReadLine()
      End  Sub
  End Module
```

Local and global variables

The function `FindAverage()` in Example 5 uses a variable called `total`. If you try to access `total` outside the subroutine, you will get a syntax error:

```
   0 references
   Sub Main()
       PrintHeading()
       Dim numbers = UserInput()
       Dim average = FindAverage(numbers)
       PrintResult(average)
       Console.WriteLine(total)
       Console.ReadLin  ⊘ ▾    'total' is not declared. It may be inaccessible due to its protection level.
   End Sub
                              Show potential fixes (Alt+Enter or Ctrl+.)
 End Module
```

`total` is not declared. It may be inaccessible due to its protection level.

Local variables

In `FindAverage()`, `total` is a **local variable**, known only in the subroutine in which it is declared. Using only local variables in a subroutine keeps it self-contained and means it can be used in many different programs without the programmer having to worry about what variable names have been used. You could have three subroutines all containing a local variable called `total` and they could hold three completely different values.

Example 6

The following program illustrates the use of local variables.

```
'Program name: Ch 8 Example 6 local variables
'program to illustrate use of local variables
Sub NameOne()
    Dim myName As String
    myName = "Alice"
    Console.WriteLine("in procedure NameOne, Name = " & myName)
End Sub
```

```
Sub NameTwo()
    Dim myName As String
    myName = "Bob"
    Console.WriteLine("in procedure NameTwo,
    Name = " & myName)
End Sub

Sub Main()
    Dim myName As String
    myName = "Kumar"
    Console.WriteLine("In main program, Name = " & myName)
    NameOne()
    Console.WriteLine("In main program, Name = " & myName)
    NameTwo()
    Console.WriteLine("In main program, Name = " & myName)
    Console.ReadLine()
End Sub
```

In each of the procedures NameOne() and NameTwo(), the variable myName is a local variable and completely separate from any variable with the same identifier used elsewhere in the program. This implements the important principle of **encapsulation**, whereby a subroutine encapsulates or holds all the variables it needs to execute and so can be used in any program without any danger of conflicting variable names.

The output from this program is:

```
In main program, Name = Kumar
in procedure NameOne, Name = Alice
In main program, Name = Kumar
in procedure NameTwo, Name = Bob
In main program, Name = Kumar
```

Global variables

A **global variable** can be used anywhere in a program, including within any functions called.

Example 7

```
Module Module1
    'Program name: Ch 8 Example 7 local and global variables
    'program to illustrate use of local and global variables
    Dim myName As String
    Sub NameOne()
        Console.WriteLine("in procedure NameOne,
        Name = " & myName)
        myName = "Alice"
        Console.WriteLine("in procedure NameOne,
        Name = " & myName)
    End Sub
```

```
      Sub NameTwo()
          myName = "Bob"
          Console.WriteLine("in procedure NameTwo,
                               Name = " & myName)
      End Sub
      Sub Main()
          myName = "Kumar"
          Console.WriteLine("In main program, Name = " & myName)
          NameOne()
          Console.WriteLine("In main program, Name = " & myName)
          NameTwo()
          Console.WriteLine("In main program, Name = " & myName)

          Console.ReadLine()
      End Sub
  End Module
```

To use `myName` in subroutine `NameOne`, for example, without passing it as a parameter, you must define it as a global variable at the head of the program, outside all the subroutines.

When it is changed in the subroutine, it is also changed in the main program and its new value is printed in the main program.

The output from this program is:

```
In main program, Name = Kumar
in procedure NameOne, Name = Kumar
in procedure NameOne, Name = Alice
In main program, Name = Alice
in procedure NameTwo, Name = Bob
In main program, Name = Bob
```

8

Q4 What will happen if you insert an extra line
```
      Console.WriteLine("in procedure NameTwo, Name = " &
      myName)
```
above the line
```
myName = "Bob"
```
in procedure `NameTwo()`?

You should generally avoid using global variables, as it can be hard to keep track of their values. Their use can cause hard-to-detect errors and make a program difficult to maintain.

Remember that subroutines should be self-contained so that the same subroutine can be used in many different programs without the programmer having to worry about whether variable names used in their program will conflict with a variable name used in the subroutine. Any values needed in the subroutine should be passed as parameters.

Exercises

1. Write a program to accept a value, representing the side of a cube, from the user and call a function to return the surface area of the cube and another function to return the volume of the cube. Display the results.

2. Write a program which asks the user to enter a short message. Call a function to encrypt the message by rearranging the letters in the sequence 2,4,6,…1,3,5…

   For example, `"Hello Jo"` will be encrypted as `"el oHloJ"`.

   Print the encoded message.

3. Write a program which asks the user to enter the average temperature for seven days of a week. Call a function which finds and returns the maximum average temperature and the day on which it occurred.

4. Write a program which asks the user to enter an employee name, hourly pay rate and the hours worked on each day of the week. Call a procedure to calculate total pay for the week, assuming time and a half on Saturdays and double time on Sundays.

   Display the employee name, total hours worked and total pay.

Chapter 9
Reading and writing files

Objectives

- Read from a text file
- Open a new file and write data to it
- Append data to an existing file
- Interrogate and process data stored in a file
- Use format operators and modifiers to format output

Storing data

When a user runs a program which asks them to type in data, the data is held in memory (RAM), and unless it is transferred to a permanent storage medium, it will be lost as soon as the program ends.

This chapter describes how to store data in a **text file** on a hard disk or another storage device so that it can be retrieved later for processing.

There are several ways of creating a text file. We can use a program to ask the user to enter the data and store it after each record has been entered. We can download data from a website and then save it in a file.

One very simple way of creating a text file is to use a text editor such as Notepad. The first exercise shows how, in a VB program, you can read a file created in this way.

Records and fields

There is a file called **films.txt** on the website **www.pgonline.co.uk** which you can download. Alternatively, you can use a text editor to type the first few records from the file and save it as **films.txt** in the same folder as your programs.

```
001,Ghostbusters,2016,PG,116,Comedy
002,The Legend of Tarzan,2016,PG,109,Action
003,Jason Bourne,2016,PG,123,Action
004,The Nice Guys,2016,R,116,Crime
005,The Secret Life of Pets,2016,G,91,Animation
006,Star Trek Beyond,2016,PG,120,Action
etc...
```

Each record in the file is typed on a new line, so six records are shown above. The end of a record is signified by an end-of-line character. You will not see the end-of-line character when you print a string, but you will see its effect, which is to move to the next line before printing.

Each record is split into **fields**, separated by commas. There are six fields in each of the records shown, and in the text file, all the fields are string fields. VB will automatically convert each string into the data type of the variable it is assigned to.

The table below is a description of each of the fields in the file:

Field name	Field type	Description
filmID	String	Unique identifier
title	String	Film title
yearReleased	Integer	Year of release
rating	String	Classification; must be G, PG or R
duration	Integer	Duration of film in minutes
genre	String	Must be Action, Animation, Fantasy, Comedy or Crime

In the real world, films are rated differently in different countries and there are more than three classifications. There are also many more genres of film, but for this purpose we will keep things simple.

Opening, reading and closing a text file

The program in Example 1 will print all the records in the file, but you cannot access individual records. To do that, you need to open the file and read the file one field at a time.

Example 1

```
Imports System.IO
' Program name: Ch 9 Example 1 read film file
Module Module1
    Sub Main()
        Dim value As String = File.ReadAllText("films.txt")
        Console.WriteLine(value)

        Console.Write("Press Enter to exit ")
        Console.ReadLine()
    End Sub
End Module
```

Note: *When you first run this program it will crash as it cannot find the file films.txt. Copy the file to the folder that the object code (.exe file) is located in. This folder location will be given in the error message and be something like:*

```
"C:\Programming\Program9-1\bin\Debug".
```

Before a file can be read or written to, it must be opened. The `FileOpen` statement assigns a channel number to the file, tells the program where the file is located, what its name is and in what **mode** it is to be opened (**Input**, **Output** or **Append**).

To assign channel number 1 to a text file named `films.txt` (held in the same folder as the object code (.exe file) of the VB program) and open it for reading:

```
FileOpen(1, "films.txt", OpenMode.Input, OpenAccess.Read)
```

When opened in read mode it is not possible to change a record or write a new record to the file.

It is good practice to close the file before exiting the program.

The program in Example 2 reads the file one field at a time. The end of the file is detected when the end-of-file marker is read.

9

Example 2

Read each record in the **films.txt** file and split it into individual fields. Print the ID, title, rating and duration of all the films having a rating "G".

```
Imports System.IO
' Program name: Ch 9 Example 2 films rated "G"
Module Module1
    Sub Main()
        Dim filmFile = 1
        Dim filmID, title, rating, genre As String
        Dim yearReleased, duration As Integer
        FileOpen(filmFile, "films.txt", OpenMode.
                Input, OpenAccess.Read)
        Do While Not EOF(filmFile)
            Input(filmFile, filmID)
            Input(filmFile, title)
            Input(filmFile, yearReleased)
            Input(filmFile, rating)
            Input(filmFile, duration)
            Input(filmFile, genre)
            If rating = "G" Then
                Console.WriteLine(filmID & " " & title &
                            " " & rating & " " & duration)
            End If
        Loop
        FileClose(filmFile)
        Console.ReadLine()
    End Sub
End Module
```

The output looks like this:

```
005 The Secret Life of Pets G 91
008 Finding Dory G 103
009 Zootopia G 108
026 The Good Dinosaur G 101
```

Example 3

Using **StreamReader**, you can read each line of a file separately.

```
Imports System.IO
' Program name: Ch 9 Example 3 read film file using
StreamReader
Module Module1
    Sub Main()
        Dim filmFile As New StreamReader("films.txt")
        Dim films As String
        films = filmFile.ReadToEnd()
        Console.WriteLine(films)
        filmFile.Close()
```

```
            Console.Write("Press Enter to exit ")
            Console.ReadLine()
        End Sub
    End Module
```

By reading each line separately with `StreamReader` it is then possible to use the Split()
method to separate the line of text into separate fields.

Example 4

Read each record in the **films.txt** file and split it into individual fields. Print the ID, title,
year released, rating, genre and duration of all the films with the genre `Comedy`.

```
Imports System.IO
' Program name: Ch 9 Example 4 read line by line using
StreamReader
Module Module1
    Sub Main()
        Dim filmID, title, rating, genre As String
        Dim yearReleased, duration As Integer
        Dim field() As String
        Dim filmFile As New StreamReader("films.txt")
        Dim filmRec As String
        Do While filmFile.Peek() <> -1
            filmRec = filmFile.ReadLine()
            field = filmRec.Split(",")
            filmID = field(0)
            title = field(1)
            yearReleased = field(2)
            rating = field(3)
            duration = field(4)
            genre = field(5)
            If genre = "Comedy" Then
                Console.WriteLine(filmID & " " & title &
                            " " & yearReleased & " " & rating &
                            " " & genre & " " & duration)
            End If
        Loop
        filmFile.Close()

        Console.Write("Press Enter to exit ")
        Console.ReadLine()
    End Sub
End Module
```

This prints:

```
001 Ghostbusters 2016 PG Comedy 116
022 The Intern 2015 PG Comedy 121
023 Ted 2 2015 R Comedy 121
024 Trainwreck 2015 R Comedy 122
029 Birdman 2014 R Comedy 119
Press Enter to exit
```

Writing to a file

New records can be written to a file by opening it in **write mode**:

```
FileOpen(filmFile, "films.txt", OpenMode.Output,
OpenAccess.Write)
```

This will create a new file. If a file named `films.txt` already exists, it will be overwritten.

Alternatively, you can open a file in **append mode:**

```
FileOpen(filmFile, "films.txt", OpenMode.Append,
OpenAccess.Write)
```

This will create a new file if none exists, or open an existing file with the file pointer at the end of the last record.

In the next example, we will create a file to hold data showing the local time and the temperature in °C of several cities around the world on a particular day in February, when it is midday in London.

The sample data to be entered is:

City	Temperature	Local time
London	7	1200
Accra	30	1200
Baghdad	20	1500
Winnipeg	-12	0600
New York	14	0700
Nairobi	27	1500
Sydney	22	2300

9

Example 5

Write a program to create a new file called **temperatures.txt**, or append records to the file if one already exists. To add the end-of-line character you need to include the system constant vbCrLf at the end of the Print string.

```
Imports System.IO
'Program name: Ch 9 Example 5 append to temperatures file
Module Module1
    Sub Main()
        Dim tempsFile = 1
        Dim city, localTime As String
        Dim temperature As Integer
        FileOpen(tempsFile, "temperatures.txt",
        OpenMode.Append, OpenAccess.Write)
        Console.WriteLine("Writes temperature data to
                          temperatures.txt")
        Console.WriteLine("If file does not exist, it will
                          be created")
        Console.Write("Enter city name, xxx to end: ")
        city = Console.ReadLine()
        Do While Not city = "xxx"
            Console.Write("Enter temperature: ")
            temperature = Console.ReadLine()
            Console.Write("Enter local time: ")
            localTime = Console.ReadLine()
            Print(tempsFile, city & "," & temperature & ",
            " & localTime & vbCrLf)
            Console.Write("Enter city name: ")
            city = Console.ReadLine()
        Loop
        FileClose(tempsFile)
        Console.Write("Press Enter to exit ")
        Console.ReadLine()
    End Sub
End Module
```

The user signals the end of input by entering `xxx`. Note that each field is separated by a comma.

Using StreamWriter

Alternatively, the same program can be written using StreamWriter. New records can be written to a file by opening it in **write mode**:

```
Dim tempsFile As New StreamWriter("temperatures.txt")
```

This will create a new file. If a file named temperatures.txt already exists, it will be overwritten.

Alternatively, you can open a file in **append mode:**

```
Dim tempsFile As New StreamWriter("temperatures.txt", True)
```

9

Example 6

Write a program that uses StreamWriter to create a new file called **temperatures.txt**, or append records to the file if one already exists.

```
Imports System.IO
' Program name: Ch 9 Example 6 writing to a file using
StreamWriter
Module Module1
    Sub Main()
        Dim tempsFile As New StreamWriter("temperatures.txt",
        True)
        Dim city, localTime As String
        Dim temperature As Integer
        Console.WriteLine("Writes data to temperatures.txt")
        Console.WriteLine("If file does not exist, it will
                        be created")
        Console.Write("Enter city name, xxx to end: ")
        city = Console.ReadLine()
        Do While Not city = "xxx"
            Console.Write("Enter temperature: ")
            temperature = Console.ReadLine()
            Console.Write("Enter local time: ")
            localTime = Console.ReadLine()
            tempsFile.WriteLiné(city & "," & temperature &
                            "," & localTime)
            Console.Write("Enter city name: ")
            city = Console.ReadLine()
        Loop
        tempsFile.Close()
        Console.Write("Press Enter to exit ")
        Console.ReadLine()
    End Sub
End Module
```

Q1 Write a program to read and print all the records in temperatures.txt.

Example 7

Read the data in the file **temperatures.txt**, convert all the Centigrade temperatures to Fahrenheit and print out both the Centigrade and Fahrenheit temperatures.

```
Imports System.IO
' Program name: Ch 9 Example 7 process temperatures file
Module Module1
    Sub Main()
        Dim tempsFile = 1
        Dim city, localTime As String
        Dim temperatureC As Integer
        Dim temperatureF As Double
```

```
        FileOpen(tempsFile, "temperatures.txt", OpenMode.Input,
                 OpenAccess.Read)
          Do While Not EOF(tempsFile)
              Input(tempsFile, city)
              Input(tempsFile, temperatureC)
              Input(tempsFile, localTime)
              temperatureF = (temperatureC * 9 / 5) + 32
              Console.WriteLine(city & " " & temperatureC & " " &
                                temperatureF & " " & localTime)
          Loop
          FileClose(tempsFile)
          Console.Write("Press Enter to exit ")
          Console.ReadLine()
      End Sub
  End Module
```

This produces the following output:

```
London 7 44.6 1200
Accra 30 86 1200
Baghdad 20 68 1500
Winnipeg -12 10.4 0600
New York 14 57.2 0700
Nairobi 27 80.6 1500
Sydney 22 71.6 2300
Press Enter to exit
```

 Suggest amendments to the above program so that both Centigrade and Fahrenheit temperatures are displayed to the nearest whole number.

Formatting output

9

The data printed above would look much better printed neatly in columns, with column headings at the top.

Format operators

To do this, VB .Net includes **format items** which are used to produce **composite formatted strings**.

The output string consists of format items and a list of arguments inserted into the output string during run-time. Using format items, instead of writing something like:

```
Console.WriteLine(city & ", " & temperatureC &
                  ", " & localTime)
```

the statement is written as

```
Console.WriteLine("{0}, {1}, {2}",
                  city, temperatureC, localTime)
```

The statement will produce the following output:

```
London, 7, 1200
```

```
Console.WriteLine("The temperature in {0} was {1:N1} degrees
                    C at {2,5}", city, temperatureC, localTime)
```

The statement will produce the following output:

```
The temperature in London was 7.0 degrees C at  1200
```

The formatting expression is divided into two parts.

The first part is the format string "The temperature in {0} was {1:N1} degrees C at {2,5}", containing one or more format items. In its simplest form, the format item consists of the index of the argument to be used. A conversion character tells the format operator what type of value is to be inserted into that position in the string. N indicates a real number. N1 indicates that the number is to be output to one decimal place.

{2,5} inserts the argument at index 2 in a field width of 5 characters. This is useful for keeping columns lined up.

The second part specifies the values (city, temperatureC, localTime) that are to be output.

> **Q3** Write statements to do the following:
> set a = 3, b = 4, c = a + b, d = a * b.
> Use format operators to print the statements
> 3 + 4 = 7
> The product of 3 and 4 is 12

Format modifiers

Format modifiers can be used to:

- specify a field width
- specify the number of digits after the decimal point
- left- or right-justify a value with a specified field width
- specify currency or a percentage

Table 9.1 shows the more common formatting conversion characters, and Table 9.2 shows the format modifiers.

Character	Example	Output format
D	{0:D}	Integer
G	{0:G}	General number
N	{0:N5}	Floating point as dd.ddddd
C	{0:C}	Currency
P	{0:P}	Percentage
d, t	{0:d} {0:t}	Date, time

Table 9.1: String formatting conversion characters

Character	Example	Description
number	{0,15}	Puts the value in a field of width 15 characters, right-justified
-	{0,-15}	Puts the value in a field of width 15 characters, left-justified
:	{0,15:N2}	Puts the value in a field of width 15 characters, with 2 decimal places
:	{0,15:P1}	Puts the value in a field of width 15 characters converted to a percentage with 1 decimal place
:	{0,15,G4}	Puts the value in a field of width 15 characters, and displays the number with the first four digits

Table 9.2: Formatting options

File processing

Often, data held in a file will need to be processed in some way. In Example 8 overleaf, data is read from the text file **temperatures.txt** into a one-dimensional array of records (structures), with each record containing the data from one row in the text file plus the calculated Fahrenheit temperature.

You can visualise this array of records as a table:

	city	temperatureC	tempF	localTime
Row 0	London	7	44.6	1200
Row 1	Accra	30	86.0	1200
Row 2	Baghdad	20	68.0	1500
etc	…	…	…..	…

The following steps are carried out:

```
for each row in the text file
  Read a row into newCityRec
  Convert the temperature to Fahrenheit
  Add the record newCityRec to the table cityTable
endfor
for each row in the table
  print individual fields
endfor
```

Example 8

Read the data in the file **temperatures.txt**, convert all the Centigrade temperatures to Fahrenheit and print out the data giving both the Centigrade and Fahrenheit temperatures.

```
'Program name: Ch 9 Example 8 process temperatures file
with struct
Module Module1
    Structure CityRec
        Dim city As String
        Dim localTime As String
        Dim temperatureC As Integer
        Dim tempF As Double
    End Structure

    Sub Main()

        Dim cityTable As New List(Of CityRec)
        Dim sortedCityTable As New List(Of CityRec)
        Dim tempsFile = 1
        FileOpen(tempsFile, "temperatures.txt",
        OpenMode.Input, OpenAccess.Read)
        Do While Not EOF(tempsFile)
            Dim newCityRec As CityRec
            Input(tempsFile, newCityRec.city)
            Input(tempsFile, newCityRec.temperatureC)
            newCityRec.tempF = (newCityRec.temperatureC *
                        9 / 5) + 32
            Input(tempsFile, newCityRec.localTime)
            cityTable.Add(newCityRec)
        Loop
        FileClose(tempsFile)
        For Each city In cityTable
            Console.WriteLine(city.city & " " &
            city.localTime & " " & city.temperatureC & " "
            & city.tempF)
        Next
        Console.Write("Press Enter to exit ")
        Console.ReadLine()
    End Sub
End Module
```

This produces the following output:

```
London 1200 7 44.6
Accra 1200 30 86
Baghdad 1500 20 68
Winnipeg 0600 -12 10.4
New York 0700 14 57.2
Nairobi 1500 27 80.6
Sydney 2300 22 71.6
```

Note: *If you are using the Console App (.NET Core) rather than (.NET Framework), you may see a recurring value of 10.39999 for Winnipeg (Temperature F). This can be resolved by using a format modifier for this field e.g.:* `{2,15:N2}`.

Example 9

Rewrite the `WriteLine` statements from Example 8 so that the data is printed in a neat tabular format.

```
Console.WriteLine("{0,-10}{1,15}{2,15}{3,15}", "City",
                "Temperature C", "Temperature F",
                "Local time")
For Each city In cityTable
    Console.WriteLine("{0,-10}{1,15}{2,15}{3,15}", city.city,
            city.temperatureC, city.tempF, city.localTime)
Next
```

This prints the data in the following format:

```
City           Temperature C   Temperature F       Local time
London                     7            44.6             1200
Accra                     30              86             1200
Baghdad                   20              68             1500
Winnipeg                 -12            10.4             0600      ...
```

Exercises

1. Write a program to write or append records to a file named `students.txt` containing student details.

   Each record will have the following fields:
   ```
   username, firstName, surname, gender, year
   ```
   Add several records to the file.

2. Open `students.txt` in read mode and output the names of all the girls in Year 10. Format the output so that it appears in columns under appropriate headings, surname followed by first name.

3. Adapt the program created in Exercise 2 so that it will ask the user to enter the year group and gender. The program will then search the file and output the names of all students that match.

Chapter 10
Databases and SQL

Objectives

- Learn how data is held in a database so that information can be easily added, deleted, amended and retrieved

- Learn some database terms: table, record, field, primary key

- Write SQL statements to create a database table and add, update or delete data in the table, and write statements to query a database

Flat file databases

A database is a collection of records held in a number of different tables. In this book, we will be concerned only with simple databases which contain just one table.

Within a database table, data is held in rows, with each row holding information about one person or thing. The data about city temperatures that we held in a text file in the last chapter could be held in a database table like this:

city	temperature	localTime
London	7	1200
Accra	30	1200
Baghdad	20	1500
Winnipeg	-12	0600
New York	14	0700
Nairobi	27	1500
Sydney	22	2300

Records, fields and primary keys

- A **record** is a row in a database table

- A **field** (also called an **attribute**) is held in a column in a database table

There are seven records, each with three fields, in the table shown on the previous page.

One of the fields is a special field known as an **identifier** or **primary key**, and this field uniquely identifies the record. In the temperatures table above, `city` is the primary key. The table cannot hold two records for the same city.

Using SQL

SQL (Structured Query Language) is a programming language that you can use to create, update and query a database. The version that you will be using with your VB.NET programs is called SQLite.

Data types

When the database table, which we will call `tblTemps`, is created, the programmer must specify what type of data is held in each field.

Data types that you will use include TEXT, INTEGER and REAL.

Data type	Description
TEXT	A text string of any length
INTEGER	A signed integer, e.g. -76, 0, 365
REAL	A floating point value, e.g. -3.7, 0.0, 56.458

Table 10.1: SQL data types

10

Creating an empty table

The SQL command to create the empty table `tblTemps` is shown below:

```
CREATE TABLE tblTemps
(
city TEXT,
temperature INTEGER,
localTime TEXT,
primary key (city)
)
```

Note: *Do not try typing this directly into VB.NET programs yet – it won't work! In the next chapter, you will learn how to put SQL statements into your programs.*

Querying a database

The most useful thing about holding data in a database is how easy it is to query the database. The syntax for a `SELECT ... FROM ... WHERE` query is:

`SELECT`   *list the fields to be displayed*

`FROM`   *specify the table where the data will come from*

`WHERE`   *list the search criteria*

`ORDER BY`   *list the fields that the results are to be sorted on (default is Ascending)*

For example, if you wanted to display the temperature and local time in Sydney (according to the simplified data held in our database), you would write:

```
SELECT  temperature, localTime
FROM  tblTemps
WHERE city = "Sydney"
```

To display all the fields in each row of the table in alphabetical order of the city, you would write:

```
SELECT  *
FROM  tblTemps
ORDER BY city
```

To display just the first five records in descending order of temperature, write:

```
SELECT  *
FROM  tblTemps
ORDER BY temperature DESC
LIMIT 5
```

Adding a record to a database table

To add a new record to an existing database table, use an `INSERT` query.

The syntax of this statement is:

```
INSERT INTO table_name (column1, column2, column3, ... columnN)
VALUES(value1, value2, value3,... valueN)
```

If you are going to enter values into every field, you do not need to specify the columns. For example,

```
INSERT INTO tblTemps
VALUES ("Montreal", -2, "0700")
```

If you wanted to enter a new record for a city but did not yet know the temperature at a particular time, you would write:

```
INSERT INTO tblTemps(city, localTime)
VALUES ("Brasilia", "0900")
```

Updating a record

To update a record, use the syntax:

```
UPDATE table_name
SET column1 = value1, column2 = value2,… columnN = valueN
WHERE [condition]
```

For example, to set the temperature in Brasilia to 20, write:

```
UPDATE tblTemps
SET temperature = 20
WHERE city = "Brasilia"
```

You can combine several conditions using the AND or OR operators.

Deleting records from a table

The syntax of the DELETE statement is:

```
DELETE FROM table_name
WHERE [condition]
```

For example, to delete all records which have temperatures below 10 and the local time is 1200, you would write:

```
DELETE FROM tblTemps
WHERE temperature < 10 AND localTime = "1200"
```

To delete all the records from the table, you would write:

```
DELETE FROM tblTemps
```

In the next chapter, you will learn how to incorporate these SQL statements into a VB.NET program.

10

Exercises

An online computer game asks players to log on before they play the game. It saves their first name, surname and player ID in a database. The database has one table called `tblScores`, which holds data in the following format:

Field name	Data type	Description
playerID	TEXT	The text string, 5 characters consisting of player's initials followed by 3 digits
firstName	TEXT	A text string of any length
surname	TEXT	A text string of any length
score1	INTEGER	Highest score achieved
score2	INTEGER	Second-highest score
score3	INTEGER	Third-highest score

1. Write an SQL statement to create the table `tblScores`.

2. Write an SQL statement to insert a new record for Maria Ferdinand, player MF123, all scores set to zero.

3. Write an SQL statement to set `score1 = 87`, `score2 = 79` and `score3 = 63` in the record for Maria Ferdinand.

4. Write an SQL statement to query the database to find the top score for Maria Ferdinand.

5. Write an SQL statement to find all the data for Maria Ferdinand.

10

Chapter 11

Using SQLite

Objectives

- Import the SQLite library into a VB.NET program
- Use SQL commands in a VB.NET program to create a database and table
- Use SQL commands to query a database and print the results of the query
- Use SQL commands to add, amend and delete records in a table
- Use a `Try … Catch` statement to trap user input errors

Using SQL commands in a VB.NET program

There are several database packages that can be imported and used in a VB.NET program, including MySQL and SQLite. **SQLite** is a simple relational database system that is supplied with VB.NET and can be imported into any VB.NET program.

Creating a database

The first thing to do is to create a new database, and within the database, create a table to hold the data.

In Chapter 9 a text file called `films.txt`, holding data about films was created. We will use the same data, this time storing it in a database table from where it can easily be queried, and have records added, updated or deleted.

First of all, the module SQLite needs to be imported.

In the Visual Studio IDE from the **Tools** menu select **NuGet Package Manager –
Manage NuGet Packages for Solution…**

In the window that opens, select the **Browse** tab and type "SQLite" in the search box.

Highlight the option System.Data.SQLite and tick the boxes for **Project** and the solution
(in this case Ch 11 Example 1).

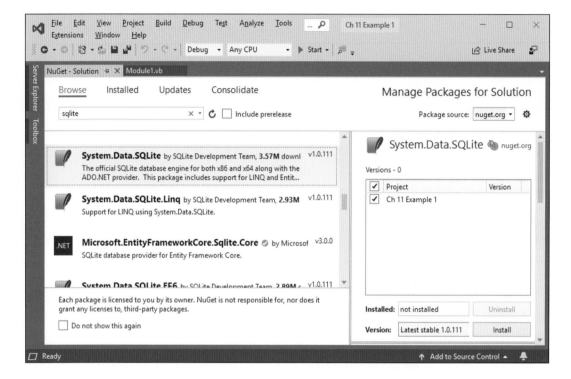

Click the **Install** button. Now wait a short while before the **Preview Changes**
window appears:

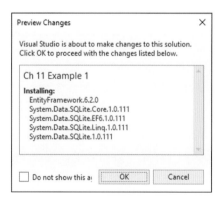

Click **OK** and accept the license. When the window shows that SQLite is installed, click
on the **Module1.vb** tab.

To use a database, a **connection object** to represent the database has to be created with the name of the file supplied as an argument. In these examples, it is assumed that the database is in the same folder as the program. If a file with this name does not exist in the folder, a new file will be created.

First, at the top of the program, import the SQLite library:

```
Imports System.Data.SQLite
```

Then, when you need to use the database, create a connection to it:

```
Dim connection As New SQLiteConnection("Data Source =
MyFilms.db")
```

Note that `connection` is just a name we chose in this example – you could call it anything, for example, `conn` or `c`.

This creates an empty database. The next thing to do is to create a table within the database.

The SQL syntax for doing this is:

```
CREATE TABLE tblFilms
(
    filmID TEXT,
    title TEXT,
    yearReleased INTEGER,
    rating TEXT,
    duration INTEGER,
    genre TEXT,
    primary key (filmID)
)
```

However, we want to do this from within the VB.NET program, so we cannot simply write SQL statements, as VB.NET will not understand.

In order to send an SQL statement to SQLite, a **command object** is required. This is a control structure used for performing all SQL commands.

The SQL command is written as a string and assigned to a variable. In the example below the variable name `sqlCommand` is used, but it could be anything.

```
Dim sqlCommand As String =
    "CREATE TABLE tblFilms (filmID TEXT,
                            title TEXT,
                            yearReleased INTEGER,
                            rating TEXT,
                            duration INTEGER,
                            genre TEXT,
                            primary key(FilmID))"
```

11

The following statement gets the command object, assigned here to a variable named cmd:

```
Dim cmd As New SQLiteCommand(SqlCommand, Connection)
```

The ExecuteNonQuery() method is needed to save the changes to the database.

Finally, you should close the connection with the statement Connection.Close()

The complete code for creating the database and the table is given below.

Example 1

```
Imports System.Data.SQLite
' Program name: Ch 11 Example 1 create films database
Module Module1
    Sub Main()
        'create or open a database called MyFilms.db
        Dim connection As New SQLiteConnection("Data Source
            = MyFilms.db")
        'SQL to create the table structure of tblFilms in
        MyFilms.db
        Dim sqlCommand As String =
            "CREATE TABLE tblFilms (filmID TEXT,
                                    title TEXT,
                                    yearReleased INTEGER,
                                    rating TEXT,
                                    duration INTEGER,
                                    genre TEXT,
                                    primary key(filmID))"
        Dim cmd As New SQLiteCommand(sqlCommand, connection)
        connection.Open()
        cmd.ExecuteNonQuery()
        connection.Close()
        Console.WriteLine("tblFilms created in MyFilms.db")
    End Sub
End Module
```

SQLite will accept either STRING or TEXT as a data type, in upper or lower case.

Note: *You can only run this program once since it creates the database and the table within it. If you want to make some changes and run it again, you must first delete the database MyFilms.db from the "…bin/Debug/" folder that Visual Studio makes for your program.*

Importing data from a text file

We could enter the film data again from scratch, but since we already have it in a text file, we can just transfer it to the database table.

Example 2

Transfer data from a text file into a database, in which a new table has already been created.

The program shown below has a short main program which calls a function `ReadTextFile()`.

Within the function `ReadTextFile()`, a connection object is created and the command object is defined.

Each row in the database table will hold one row from the text file, split into its individual fields.

The SQL command uses parameters (identifiers starting with @), which get values set with the command `cmd.Parameters.AddWithValue()`.

A `cmd.ExecuteNonQuery()` method is used to write the record to the database table.

```
Imports System.Data.SQLite
'Program name: Ch 11 Example 2 transfer film records
'transfer records to film database from text file
Module Module1
    Function ReadTextFile() As Integer
        Dim connection As New SQLiteConnection("Data Source
                    = MyFilms.db")
        Dim cmd As New SQLiteCommand(Connection)
        Dim sqlCommand As String
        Dim numRecs = 0
        Dim filmID, title, rating, genre As String
        Dim yearReleased, duration As Integer
        Dim filmFile = 1
        sqlCommand = "INSERT INTO tblFilms VALUES (@filmID,
                    @title, @yearRelased, @rating,
                    @duration, @genre);"
        cmd.CommandText = sqlCommand
        connection.Open()
        FileOpen(filmFile, "films.txt", OpenMode.Input,
        OpenAccess.Read)
        Do While Not EOF(filmFile)
            NumRecs += 1
            Input(filmFile, filmID)
            Input(filmFile, title)
            Input(filmFile, yearReleased)
            Input(filmFile, rating)
            Input(filmFile, duration)
            Input(filmFile, genre)
```

```
            Console.WriteLine(filmID & " " & title & " " &
                    yearReleased & " " & rating & " " &
                    duration & " " & genre)
            ' Insert this record into the database
            cmd.Parameters.AddWithValue("@filmID", FilmID)
            cmd.Parameters.AddWithValue("@title", Title)
            cmd.Parameters.AddWithValue("@yearRelased",
                                        yearReleased)
            cmd.Parameters.AddWithValue("@rating", rating)
            cmd.Parameters.AddWithValue("@duration", duration)
            cmd.Parameters.AddWithValue("@Genre", genre)
            cmd.ExecuteNonQuery()
        Loop
        FileClose(filmFile)
        connection.Close()
        Return numRecs
    End Function

    Sub Main()
        Dim numRecs As Integer = ReadTextFile()
        Console.WriteLine()
        Console.WriteLine(numRecs & " records transferred")
        Console.Write("Press Enter to Exit")
        Console.ReadLine()
    End Sub
End Module
```

A count is kept in the function `ReadTextFile()` of the number of records transferred, and this is printed in the main program.

11) Creating a new database and loading it with data

There are several ways of getting data into a database table. We have seen in Example 2 how you can transfer data from a text file. In the next example, we define a new database to hold the temperature in different cities at a given time, in an array of tuples called **temps**. We'll use the same data that we used in Chapter 10.

Example 3

Create a new database named **CityTemperatures.db**, and within this database, a table named **tblTemps**. Define a list of tuples, each of which holds the data for one record. Use an SQL command to insert records into the table.

```
Imports System.Data.SQLite
'Program name: Ch 11 Example 3 populate tblTemps
'Creates a table called tblTemps in database
'CityTemperatures.db
'then adds temperatures for several cities to tblTemps
Module Module1
```

```vbnet
Sub CreateTable()
    Dim connection As New SQLiteConnection("Data Source
    = CityTemperatures.db")
    Dim cmd As New SQLiteCommand(connection)
    'SQL to create the table structure
    Dim sqlCommand As String =
        "CREATE TABLE tblTemps(City TEXT,
                               Temperature INTEGER,
                               LocalTime TEXT,
                               primary key(City))"
    cmd.CommandText = sqlCommand
    connection.Open()
    'save table structure
    cmd.ExecuteNonQuery()
    connection.Close()
End Sub

Function InputData() As Integer
    Dim temps = {("London", 7, "1200"),
                 ("Accra", 30, "1200"),
                 ("Baghdad", 20, "1500"),
                 ("Winnipeg", -12, "0600"),
                 ("New York", 14, "0700"),
                 ("Nairobi", 27, "1500"),
                 ("Sydney", 22, "2300")}

    Dim connection As New SQLiteConnection("Data Source
                                = CityTemperatures.db")
    Dim sqlCommand As String
    sqlCommand = "INSERT INTO tblTemps VALUES (@City,
                @Temperature, @LocalTime)"
    Dim cmd As New SQLiteCommand(connection)
    cmd.CommandText = sqlCommand
    Dim numRecs = 0
    Dim totalRecs As Integer
    totalRecs = temps.Count()
    connection.Open()
    For i = 0 To totalRecs - 1
        With temps(i)
            numRecs += 1
            'set tuple values as parameters
            cmd.Parameters.AddWithValue("@City", .Item1)
            cmd.Parameters.AddWithValue("@Temperature",
                                        .Item2)
            cmd.Parameters.AddWithValue("@LocalTime",
                                        .Item3)
            ' Insert this record into the database
            cmd.ExecuteNonQuery()
        End With
    Next
    connection.Close()
    Return numRecs
End Function
```

```
Sub Main()
    'create or open database and create table
    CreateTable()
    Dim numRecs As Integer = InputData()
    Console.WriteLine()
    Console.WriteLine(numRecs & " records transferred")
    Console.WriteLine()
    Console.Write("Press Enter to Exit")
    Console.ReadLine()
End Sub
End Module
```

Querying the database

To make a query and print the results, use normal SQL syntax to define the query and then write a statement to make the command object execute the SQL.

The first example shows how to print all the records in the **CityTemperatures** database.

Example 4: Print the records in tblTemps

```
Imports System.Data.SQLite
'Program name: Ch 11 Example 4 print tblTemps
Module Module1
    Sub Main()
        'open database
        Dim connection As New SQLiteConnection("Data Source
        = CityTemperatures.db")
        connection.Open()
        Dim sqlCommand As String
        sqlCommand = "SELECT * FROM tblTemps ORDER BY
        Temperature DESC"
        Dim cmd As New SQLiteCommand(connection)
        cmd.CommandText = sqlCommand
        Dim reader As SQLiteDataReader = cmd.ExecuteReader()
        While reader.Read()
            Console.WriteLine(reader("City") & ", " &
                              reader("Temperature") & ", " &
                              reader("LocalTime"))
        End While
        reader.Close()
        connection.Close()
        Console.WriteLine()
        Console.Write("Press Enter to Exit")
        Console.ReadLine()
    End Sub
End Module
```

The output is as follows:

```
Accra, 30, 1200
Nairobi, 27, 1500
Sydney, 22, 2300
Baghdad, 20, 1500
New York, 14, 0700
London, 7, 1200
Winnipeg, -12, 0600
```

Example 5: Limiting the number of records output

You can specify how many records you want to output using the LIMIT parameter.

As with a text file, you can format the output neatly in columns (see Tables 9.1 and 9.2).

```
Imports System.Data.SQLite
'Program name: Ch 11 Example 5 print 5 recs in tblTemps
Module Module1
    Sub Main()
        'open database
        Dim connection As New SQLiteConnection("Data Source
                    = CityTemperatures.db")
        connection.Open()
        Dim sqlCommand As String
        sqlCommand = "SELECT * FROM tblTemps ORDER BY
                    Temperature DESC LIMIT 5"
        Dim cmd As New SQLiteCommand(connection)
        cmd.CommandText = sqlCommand
        Dim reader As SQLiteDataReader = cmd.ExecuteReader()
        Console.WriteLine("{0,-15}{1,20}{2,20}", "City",
                    "Temperature", "Local time")
        While reader.Read()
            Console.WriteLine("{0,-15}{1,16:D}
            {2,21}", reader("City"), reader("Temperature"),
            reader("LocalTime"))
        End While
        reader.Close()
        connection.Close()
        Console.WriteLine()
        Console.Write("Press Enter to Exit")
        Console.ReadLine()
    End Sub
End Module
```

11

This produces output:

```
City                 Temperature         Local time
Accra                     30                1200
Nairobi                   27                1500
Sydney                    22                2300
Baghdad                   20                1500
New York                  14                0700
```

Example 6: Specifying conditions

You can specify a condition to determine which records will be selected. For example, you could output all cities with temperatures of 25 or more.

```
Imports System.Data.SQLite
'Program name: Ch 11 Example 6 print temps 25 or more
Module Module1
    Sub Main()
        Dim connection As New SQLiteConnection("Data Source
                    = CityTemperatures.db")
        connection.Open()
        Dim sqlCommand As String
        sqlCommand = "SELECT city, temperature
                    FROM tblTemps WHERE temperature >= 25
                    ORDER BY temperature DESC"
        Dim cmd As New SQLiteCommand(connection)
        cmd.CommandText = sqlCommand
        Dim reader As SQLiteDataReader = cmd.ExecuteReader()
        Console.WriteLine("{0,-15}{1,20}", "City",
                    "Temperature")
        While reader.Read()
            Console.WriteLine("{0,-15}{1,16:D}",
                    reader("city"), reader("temperature"))
        End While
        reader.Close()
        connection.Close()
        Console.WriteLine()
        Console.Write("Press Enter to Exit")
        Console.ReadLine()
    End Sub
End Module
```

Adding records entered by the user

Often, a user will need to add, amend or delete a record from the database.

Example 7: Add records to the temperatures database

Write a program to allow the user to enter several records into the temperature database.

- First, the SQLite module is imported and a connection object and a command object are created, as before.

- The SQL statement is written using parameters.

- The While loop is entered, allowing the user to enter data which is added to the command object via parameters.

- The data is inserted into the database using the ExecuteNonQuery() method.

- The loop continues until the user enters "n".

- The connection is closed.

```vbnet
Imports System.Data.SQLite
Module Module1
    Sub Main()
        'open database
        Dim connection As New SQLiteConnection("Data Source
                      = CityTemperatures.db")
        Dim cmd As New SQLiteCommand(connection)
        connection.Open()
        cmd.CommandText = "INSERT INTO tblTemps
                      VALUES(@city,@temperature,@localTime)"
        Dim enterAnotherCity = True
        While enterAnotherCity
            Console.Write("Enter city name: ")
            Dim city = Console.ReadLine()
            Console.Write("Enter temperature: ")
            Dim temperature As Integer = Console.ReadLine()
            Console.Write("Enter local time: ")
            Dim localTime = Console.ReadLine()
            cmd.Parameters.AddWithValue("@city", city)
            cmd.Parameters.AddWithValue("@temperature",
                                        temperature)
            cmd.Parameters.AddWithValue("@localTime",
                                        localTime)
            Try
                cmd.ExecuteNonQuery()
            Catch
                Console.WriteLine("A record for this city
                            already exists")
            End Try
            Console.Write("Enter another city (y/n)? ")
            If Console.ReadLine() = "n" Then
                enterAnotherCity = False
            End If
        End While
        connection.Close()
        Console.WriteLine()
        Console.Write("Press Enter to Exit")
        Console.ReadLine()
    End Sub
End Module
```

Error handling

If the user enters the name of a city which is already in the database, the program will crash, because `City` is a key field, which has to be unique in a database table.

Example 8

In order to prevent this happening, you can include a `Try…Catch` clause. In the code above, replace the statement:

```
cmd.ExecuteNonQuery()
```

with

```
Try
    cmd.ExecuteNonQuery()
Catch
    Console.WriteLine("A record for this city already exists")
End Try
```

This works as follows:

- first, the statement between the `Try` and `Catch` statements is executed

- if no exception occurs, the `Catch` clause is skipped and execution of the `Try` statement is finished

- if an exception occurs, the `Catch` clause is executed

Deleting a record

In Example 9, the main program calls a procedure to delete a record, passing it the name of the database.

There is no need to use the `Try…Catch` clause here because the program will not crash if you enter the name of a city that does not exist.

The function deletes the record if it is present and then outputs the contents of the database – this is useful for testing but could be removed from a finished application.

Example 9: Delete a record from the temperatures database

```
Imports System.Data.SQLite
'Program name: Ch 11 Example 9 deleting a record
Module Module1
    Sub DeleteRec(dBname As String)
        Dim connectionString As String = "Data Source = "
        & dBname
        Dim connection As New
        SQLiteConnection(connectionString)
        Dim cmd As New SQLiteCommand(connection)
        connection.Open()
        Console.Write("Enter name of city to delete: ")
        Dim myCity = Console.ReadLine()
        cmd.CommandText = "DELETE FROM tblTemps WHERE City =
                          '" & myCity & "'"
        cmd.ExecuteNonQuery()
        cmd.CommandText = "SELECT * FROM tblTemps ORDER BY
                          Temperature DESC"
```

```
        Dim reader As SQLiteDataReader = cmd.ExecuteReader()
        Console.WriteLine("{0,-15}{1,20}{2,20}", "City",
                      "Temperature", "Local time")
        While reader.Read()
            Console.WriteLine("{0,-15}{1,16:D}{2,21}",
            reader("city"), reader("temperature"),
            reader("localTime"))
        End While
        reader.Close()
        connection.Close()
    End Sub
    Sub Main()
        DeleteRec("CityTemperatures.db")
        Console.Write("Press Enter to Exit")
        Console.ReadLine()
    End Sub
End Module
```

If the `myCity` value is not in the table, no error is indicated when an attempt is made to delete the record.

Updating the database

The SQL statement to update the temperature in a given city, for example, London, from its current value of 7°C to 10°C is:

```
UPDATE tblTemps
SET temperature = 10
WHERE city = "London"
```

However, in a VB program, you will probably want to allow the user to enter the field to be used in the search condition, and the value to which it is to be set. In that case, you need to replace the literal values specified above with string variables containing the data entered by the user. This is shown in the following example.

Example 10: Amend a value in the database table

Write a program to ask the user which field in the table they wish to amend, and what the new value is to be. Update the record accordingly.

```
Imports System.Data.SQLite
'Program name: Ch 11 Example 10 amend CityTemperatures record
Module Module1
    Sub PrintRecords(cmd)
        cmd.CommandText = "SELECT * FROM tblTemps"
        Dim reader As SQLiteDataReader = cmd.ExecuteReader()
        Console.WriteLine("{0,-15}{1,20}{2,20}",
                      "City", "Temperature",
                      "Local time")
```

```
                While reader.Read()
                    Console.WriteLine("{0,-15}{1,16:D}{2,21}",
                            reader("city"), reader("temperature"),
                            reader("localTime"))
                End While
                reader.Close()
        End Sub

        Sub Amend()
            Dim connectionString = "Data Source =
                                    CityTemperatures.db"
            Dim connection As New
            SQLiteConnection(connectionString)
            Dim cmd As New SQLiteCommand(connection)
            connection.Open()
            printRecords(cmd)
            Console.Write("Enter city name of the record
                        to amend: ")
            Dim keyField As String = Console.ReadLine()
            keyField = "'" & keyField & "'"
            Console.Write("Change which field (Temperature or
                        LocalTime)? ")
            Dim field As String = Console.ReadLine()
            Console.Write("Enter the new value for this field: ")
            Dim newValue = Console.ReadLine()
            newValue = "'" & newValue & "'"
            Try
                cmd.CommandText = "UPDATE tblTemps SET " &
                    field & " = " & newValue & "
                    WHERE City =              " & keyField
                cmd.ExecuteNonQuery()
                Console.WriteLine("Record updated")
            Catch
                Console.WriteLine("No record updated - invalid
                                data entered")
            End Try
            PrintRecords(cmd)
            connection.Close()
        End Sub

        Sub Main()
            Amend()
            Console.Write("Press Enter to Exit")
            Console.ReadLine()
        End Sub
    End Module
```

If the data input by the user for `keyField` or `field` does not exist, the exception handling stops the program from crashing and no change is made to the data.

Exercises

Use the Films.db database for these exercises.

1. Write a program to print all the records in Films.db.

2. Write a program to do the following:

    Display a menu of options.

    ```
    1. Add a record
    2. Delete a record
    3. Amend a record
    4. Print all records
    5. Exit
    ```
    Implement each of these options as a subroutine.

3. Write a program to do the following:

    Display a menu of options.

    ```
    1. Print details of all films
    2. Print all films of a particular genre
    3. Print Film titles, ratings and genre sequenced by genre
       and rating
    4. Print details of all films released in 2016, sequenced
       by title
    5. Exit
    ```

    Implement each of these options as a subroutine.

11

Chapter 12

Introduction to the graphical user interface

Objectives

- Create a simple Windows Forms app in the IDE
- Create a form with buttons and label widgets
- Set the size and colour of a Windows form
- Learn how to change properties of widgets

Creating a Windows Forms App

Launch Visual Studio and choose **Create a new project**.

Search for **forms** and select **Windows Forms App (.NET Framework)**. Make sure you select the Visual Basic version if there is more than one version. Then click **Next**.

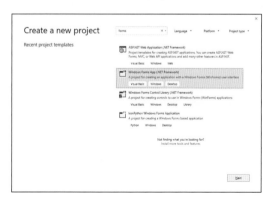

Choose the folder location where you want to save your programs and give a name to both the project and solution.

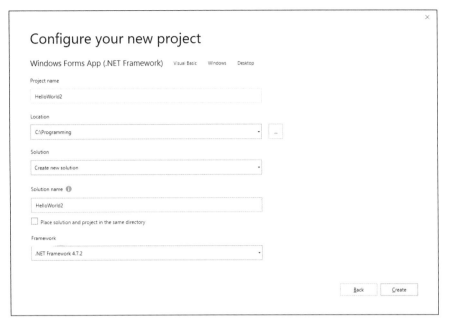

Click **Create**. This opens the IDE window:

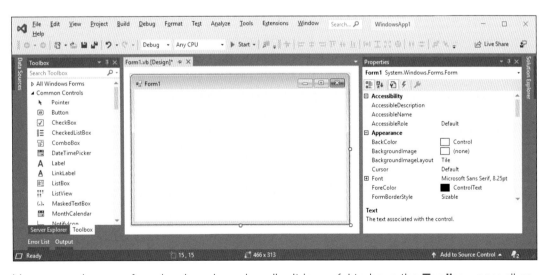

You can resize your form by dragging a handle. It is useful to have the **Toolbox** as well as the **Properties window** visible while working on the form. If the Toolbox is missing press **CTRL-ALT-X**. If the Properties window is missing, press **F4**.

Controls

Controls are GUI objects, such as buttons and text entry fields, that are used to interface with the program. They can also be used to display information to the user in the form of a label or a graphic. When adding a control to the form designer, it is a good idea to give it a sensible name, so that your program code will be easier to maintain. The convention is to use a prefix with each control identifier that represents the control's type. For example, the identifier for a confirm button might be `btnConfirm`.

Here is a list of prefixes for some common components along with an example:

Components	Prefix	Example
Button	`btn`	`btnConfirm`
Checkbox	`chk`	`chkSunday`
Form	`frm`	`frmConfirmation`
Label	`lbl`	`lblInstructions`
Textbox	`txt`	`txtFirstName`
ComboBox	`cbo`	`cboTasks`
GroupBox	`grp`	`grpDeliveryMethod`

The "Hello World" program

Example 1

Select the **Label** component from the **toolbox** and drag it onto the form.

In the **Properties** window change the **Text** property to "`Hello World`".

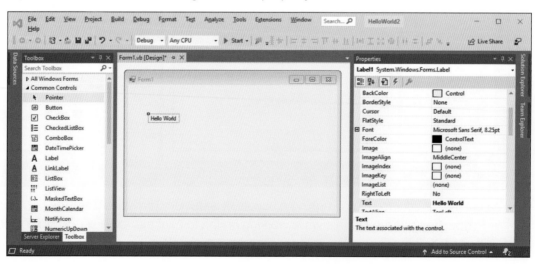

Click on the **Start** button ▶ Start ▾ on the IDE toolbar. A window like this will appear:

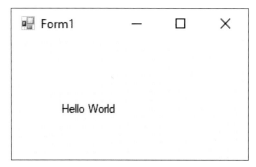

You can click and drag the edges to resize the window and drag the window around the screen.

Adding and editing a button component

Select the **Button** component from the toolbox and drag it onto the form.

In the **Design** section of the **Properties** window change the **Name** from **Button1** to **btnClickMe**.

All components have specific properties associated with them, and a button has a text property which can be used to display the text on a button:

In the **Appearance** section of the **Properties** window change the **Text** property to **"Click me"**.

If you run this form, nothing happens when the button is clicked because we have not specified any action.

Double-click the button in the form design window. This opens the Form1.vb window. The subroutine header and end is already provided for you and you only need to add the statements that you want to execute when the button is clicked.

You can change the text on the button by specifying the new text:

```
Public Class Form1
    Private Sub btnClickMe_Click(sender As Object,
            e As EventArgs) Handles btnClickMe.Click
        btnClickMe.Text = "Click here"
    End Sub
End Class
```

Run this form and you will see the window change:

Note: When you load examples you may find that the form designer doesn't show. If so, press **Shift-F7** to show the **Designer** view. Alternatively, open **Solution Explorer** and double-click `Form1.vb`.

Responding to user input

Example 2

The sample program opens a window with a label and two buttons:

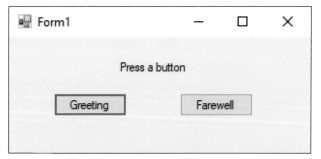

When a button is pressed, the text on the label changes:

12

On a blank form add the following components and change the property values as shown in the table:

Widget	Property	Value
Button1	Name	btnGreeting
	Text	Greeting
Button2	Name	btnFarewell
	Text	Farewell
Label1	Name	lblMessage
	Text	Press a button

```
'Ch 12 Example 2 hello goodbye
Public Class Form1
    Private Sub btnClickMe_Click(sender As Object,
                e As EventArgs) Handles btnGreeting.Click
        lblMessage.Text = "Hello!"
    End Sub

    Private Sub btnFarewell_Click(sender As Object, e As
            EventArgs) Handles btnFarewell.Click
        lblMessage.Text = "Goodbye!"
    End Sub
End Class
```

Setting Form properties

You can set the size and colour of the window and specify whether it should be resizable.

Example 3

Amend the form for Example 2, adjusting the properties as shown below:

Widget	Property	Value	Comment
	Name	frmGreeting	Identifier
	BackColor	ActiveCaption	Light blue background
	FormBorderStyle	FixedSingle	Window not resizable
Form1	Text	Demo	Text in header
	Size	200, 150	Size of window
	MaximizeBox	False	Window cannot be maximised
	MinimizeBox	False	Window cannot be minimised

You can also set the size, position and font size of the widgets.

Widget	Property	Value
Button1	Name	btnGreeting
	Text	Greeting
	Size	75, 25
	Location	10, 70
Button2	Name	btnFarewell
	Text	Farewell
	Size	75, 25
	Location	100, 70
Label1	Name	lblMessage
	Text	Press a button
	Font Size	12
	Location	40, 30

The window will now appear like this:

Exercises

12

1. Develop a Windows Forms app to place a button saying "Click here" in a window. When the button is clicked, a message "Hi there!" appears under the button. Give the window a title "Placing a button".

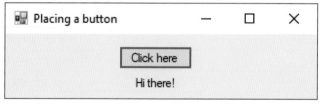

2. (a) Develop a Windows Forms app to display, in a light green window size 200 x 120, two buttons saying "Left" and "Right". Under the buttons, display a label saying "left" when the "left" button is pressed, or "right" when the "right" button is pressed. Use the Size and Location properties to place the widgets neatly spaced in the window.

   (b) Centre the text in the label. Use the TextAlign property for alignment and change AutoSize to False to change the label size.

Chapter 13

Developing a Windows application

Objectives

- Design and implement a data entry form for a given application
- Implement actions to be performed when a button is clicked
- Use a message window to give information to the user
- Close the window and end the program

Sample application 1

This chapter describes how you might set about developing a GUI application using a Windows Form. The sample application will display a data entry screen to enable a teacher or administrator to enter a user ID, first name and surname for a student.

Designing the data input window

You should start by hand-drawing a rough design for your form, perhaps something like the image below.

Using group boxes

In the hand-drawn design, the form has been divided into three distinct areas – the heading, the input boxes and the buttons. The diagram shows that the username, first name and surname will need to be held in their own group box. The buttons and heading will not be in a group box; they will be in the main window.

Using group boxes is useful because it means that everything contained in the group box can be moved as one, without affecting any other components. You can also choose to make the background colour of the group box different from the window.

Building the form

The components that will be needed for the form are as follows:

Component	Identifier	Description
Label1		Form heading
GroupBox1		Frame around the text labels and input fields
Label2		Label "Username"
Label3		Label "First name"
Label4		Label "Surname"
TextBox1	txtUsername	Data entry box
TextBox2	txtFirstName	Data entry box
TextBox3	txtSurname	Data entry box
Button1	btnSubmit	Button to submit data
Button2	btnClear	Button to clear entry boxes

Table 13.1: Components required for the program

In general, as you never need to change or move labels once they are placed, there is no need to name them.

When data for a student has been entered, the user will submit it by pressing a **Submit** button. This will cause the data to be output, and the user can click a **Clear** button to clear the fields ready to enter data for the next person. Once all data has been entered, the user can end the program by closing the window.

13

Creating the Windows form

First, create a new Windows Forms project and add in one label, a group box and two buttons. The **GroupBox** is found in the **Containers** section of the **Toolbox**.

Now drag three further labels into the group box. Update the properties of each component so that they match those in the screenshot below.

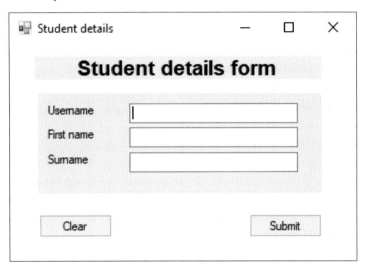

13

Values for key properties are given below:

Component	Property	Value
Form1	Text	Student details
GroupBox1	Text	""
	BackColor	224, 224, 224
Label1 (for the heading)	BackColor	244, 244, 224
	Text	Student details form
	Font	Arial; 16pt; Bold
	Autosize	False
	TextAlign	MiddleCenter
Label2 (Username)	Text	Username
Label3 (First name)	Text	First name
Label4 (Surname)	Text	Surname
TextBox1 (Username)	Name	txtUsername
TextBox2 (First name)	Name	txtFirstName
TextBox3 (Surname)	Name	txtSurname
Button1	Name	btnSubmit
	Text	Submit
Button2	Name	btnClear
	Text	Clear

Notice that as there will be no need to refer to the labels, therefore, we do not need to give them identifier names. It doesn't matter if you do choose to give them identifier names, but it is not necessary to do so.

The Submit and Clear button click event subroutines

Double-click on each button to get the subroutine headings. Then complete the code as shown.

The Clear button assigns the Text property for each text box an empty string (""). It then sets the focus to the first text box ready for the next username to be entered.

The Submit button gets the user input from the text box and outputs it to the console window. In a more realistic application, these fields could be written to a file or database for later retrieval.

```vb
Public Class Form1
    Private Sub BtnClear_Click(sender As Object,
                e As EventArgs) Handles btnClear.Click
        txtUsername.Text = ""
        txtFirstName.Text = ""
        txtSurname.Text = ""
        txtUsername.Focus()
    End Sub
```

```
    Private Sub BtnSubmit_Click(sender As Object,
                              e As EventArgs)
                              Handles btnSubmit.Click
        Console.WriteLine("Username: " & txtUsername.Text)
        Console.WriteLine("First name: " & txtFirstName.Text)
        Console.WriteLine("Surname: " & txtSurname.Text)
    End Sub
End Class
```

You can view the output after pressing the **Submit** button by selecting the **Output** pane.

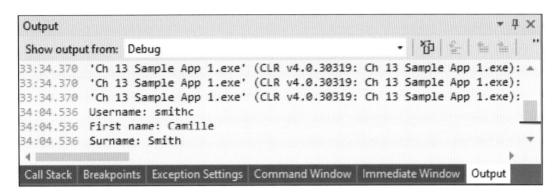

When the submit button is clicked, the details are output in the Output pane, but the text boxes are not cleared. As the handler for BtnClear_Click already clears the textboxes, this can be called at the end of the BtnSubmit_Click handler as follows:

```
    Private Sub BtnSubmit_Click(sender As Object,
                              e As EventArgs)
                              Handles btnSubmit.Click
        Console.WriteLine("Username: " & txtUsername.Text)
        Console.WriteLine("First name: " & txtFirstName.Text)
        Console.WriteLine("Surname: " & txtSurname.Text)
        BtnClear_Click(sender, e)
    End Sub
```

Sample application 2

In this application, the user will log on by typing a username and password. If the password is incorrect, an error message will be displayed, the username field and the password will be cleared and the user can press a **Password hint** button to help them remember their password. In this example, the password is "aaaaaa". The username is not checked. The input screen looks like this:

Once the password has been entered correctly, another message window is displayed

111

inviting the user to continue. Once they press **OK**, the message window and the main window close. In this example, the program simply prints "carry on now…" and ends.

Create a new **Windows Forms App** project and add the following components to the form. Set their **properties** as follows:

Component	Property	Value
Form1	Text	Login Screen
	Text	" "
	BackColor	224, 224, 224
Label1	Text	Username
Label2	Text	Password
Label3	Name	lblMessageAlert
	Autosize	False
	TextAlign	TopCenter
	Text	" "
TextBox1	Name	txtUsername
TextBox2	Name	txtPassword
	UseSystemPasswordChar	True
Button1	Name	btnSubmit
	Text	Submit
Button2	Name	btnHint
	Text	Hint

The password typed by the user will be replaced by the standard system password character on the screen, as a security measure.

Using a message box

A **message box** is useful for alerting the user to an error or to give them information. In this application, we will use two message boxes. The first one pops up with a message when they press a **Password hint** button if they have forgotten their password. It is common practice in many login routines to include a button to click if you have forgotten your password – normally the system will reset the password and email you a new one.

The VB code to display the message box is:

```
MessageBox.Show("Hint: Try password aaaaaa", "Password
            hint", MessageBoxButtons.OK,
            MessageBoxIcon.Information)
```

This generates the pop-up window, and the user must click **OK** to continue. This code is placed inside the handler for the **Hint** button.

Once the user presses the **Submit** button, the program checks the password and if correct, displays a message "Password accepted" and a message box to allow the user to continue.

Closing the Windows form

The form named `Form1` is closed in the `btnSubmit_Click` subroutine with the statement:

```
Close()

Public Class Form1
    Private Sub BtnSubmit_Click(sender As Object,
                e As EventArgs) Handles btnSubmit.Click
        If txtPassword.Text <> "aaaaaa" Then
            lblMessageAlert.Text = "Password incorrect"
            txtUsername.Text = ""
            txtPassword.Text = ""
            txtUsername.Focus()
        Else
            lblMessageAlert.Text = "Password accepted"
            Console.WriteLine("password accepted")
            Console.WriteLine("Usernam: " & txtUsername.Text)
            Console.WriteLine("Password: " & txtPassword.Text)
            MessageBox.Show("Press OK to continue",
                        "Password OK", MessageBoxButtons.OK,
                        MessageBoxIcon.Information)
            Console.WriteLine("carry on now...")
            Close()
        End If
    End Sub

    Private Sub BtnHint_Click(sender As Object, e As
                EventArgs) Handles btnHint.Click
        MessageBox.Show("Hint: Try password aaaaaa",
                    "Password hint", MessageBoxButtons.OK,
                    MessageBoxIcon.Information)
    End Sub
End Class
```

Sample application 3

This application allows a user (for example, a teacher) to create a multiple-choice test consisting of several questions which could be saved in a text file or database. The input window will look like this:

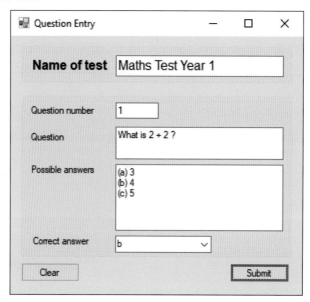

Create a new **Windows Forms App** project and add the following components to the form. The values for key **properties** are shown below.

Component	Property	Value
Form1	Text	Question entry
	BackColor	192, 255, 255
GroupBox1	Text	" "
	BackColor	224, 224, 224
Label1	Text	Name of test
	Font	Arial, 12pt, Bold
TextBox1	Name	txtTestName
GroupBox2	Text	" "
	BackColor	224, 224, 224
Label2	Text	Question number
Label3	Text	Question
Label 4	Text	Possible answers
Label5	Text	Correct answer:
TextBox2	Name	txtQuestionNumber

Textbox3	Name	txtQuestion
	Multiline	True
TextBox4	Name	txtPossibleAnswers
	Multiline	True
ComboBox1	Name	cboCorrectAnswer
	Items	a
		b
		c
Button1	Name	btnSubmit
	Text	Submit
Button2	Name	btnClear
	Text	Clear

The following code is used for the button handlers:

```
Public Class Form1
    Private Sub BtnSubmit_Click(sender As Object, e As
    EventArgs) Handles btnSubmit.Click
        Console.WriteLine("Test name " & txtTestName.Text)
        Console.WriteLine("Question number: " &
                         txtQuestionNumber.Text)
        Console.WriteLine("Question: " & txtQuestion.Text)
        Console.WriteLine("Possible answers: ")
        Console.WriteLine(txtPossibleAnswers.Text)
        Console.WriteLine("Correct answer: " &
                         cboCorrectAnswer.Text)
        Console.WriteLine()
        BtnClear_Click(sender, e)
    End Sub
    Private Sub BtnClear_Click(sender As Object, e As
    EventArgs) Handles btnClear.Click
        txtQuestionNumber.Text = ""
        txtQuestion.Text = ""
        txtPossibleAnswers.Text = ""
        cboCorrectAnswer.Text = ""
        txtQuestionNumber.Focus()
    End Sub
End Class
```

Note: *In this program, the questions entered are not stored in a file, they are just output to the output pane. Normally you would save them in a file or database so that the test could be read at a later date by someone sitting the test.*

Exercises

1. Amend Sample Application 1 so that the program stores student details in a text file or database file.

2. Write a program to retrieve and print the details for a student with a username entered by the user.

3. Write a program which allows a user to choose a username and password. The password must be at least 6 characters, in which case a message "password accepted" is displayed. Otherwise, a message "Password must be at least 6 characters" is displayed and the fields are cleared for the user to re-enter their username and password.

4. Amend the program in Sample Application 3 to store the test in a text file instead of printing the questions. Test your program by entering at least 3 questions.

Chapter 14

Program design

Objectives

- To identify the major tasks to be performed in a solution to a given problem
- To plan the structure of the program
- To split the program into a number of self-contained subroutines

Planning a program

As the requirements of a system become more complex, it becomes essential to plan out a solution on paper before starting to write code. There are various 'tools' you can use to help with this, including:

- structure diagrams
- pseudocode
- flowcharts

You may have covered these tools in another part of your course. In this chapter, we will look at a sample task and plan a solution by breaking the problem down into its component parts or subtasks. Once we have planned the solution, subroutines or functions for each subtask can be coded.

The sample task

In Sample application 3 in the previous chapter, we looked at how to write a program to allow a teacher to enter questions for a multiple-choice test. We will expand the problem in this chapter to start by presenting a menu of options, allowing the teacher to create a new test, add to an existing test, print the contents of a test file or edit a particular question. The test will be stored in a text file.

Step 1 – Identify the major tasks

We can identify several tasks that need to be performed in the program. Start by writing a list, and then look at how the program can be split up into different self-contained subroutines, with the main program which calls the subroutines. A first attempt might look like this:

```
Display the menu
Get the user choice and validate it
Create a new file and add questions
Append questions to an existing file
Edit an existing question
Print contents of file
```

Step 2 – Add a structure to incorporate these functions

Many programs will have a number of different options from which the user can choose. This is usually achieved by displaying a menu and asking the user to choose an option, which is then validated. We can visualise that the menu would look something like this:

```
Option 1: Create a new test file
Option 2: Add questions to an existing test
Option 3: Edit questions in an existing test
Option 4: Print the contents of a test file
Option 5: Quit
Please enter your choice:
```

The program will display the menu, get the user choice, validate it, and carry out the chosen option.

We can express this structure in **pseudocode,** which uses statements and structures similar to those that you may use in VB but without paying attention to the syntax of a particular language. A possible outline structure is shown below:

```
choice = None
display menu
call function getMenuChoice to get and validate choice
if choice = "1"
   call subroutine to create new file
else if choice = "2"
   call subroutine to open existing file
   call subroutine to accept user input and write to file
```

```
else if choice = "3"
   call subroutine to edit question and write to file
else if choice = "4"
   call subroutine to print the file
endif
if file has been opened
   close the file
endif
print goodbye message
```

Step 3 – Add more detail where required

Next, you need to decide whether the program should use a GUI or a text interface. Once you have made a decision, you can either use pseudocode to plan the logic, or it may be easier just to start coding.

To code the program, you could first create the main program, which displays the menu, calls a function to get and validate the choice, and then calls a different subroutine depending on the choice. For each of these subroutines, write a "stub"; e.g. the subroutine heading and **an output** statement – for example,

```
Sub EditQuestions():
Console.WriteLine("Option 3 Edit questions chosen")
```

This will demonstrate that the subroutine has been called at the correct point in the logic, and the processing can be added later on.

Get that working correctly, and then code each function in turn.

Exercises

1. (a) Design a structured program which displays a menu of shapes. The user then inputs the name of a shape, which could be either "circle" or "rectangle", together with either the radius or the length of each side. The program calculates its area and prints it.

   (b) Write the program as a series of subroutines. (Use the formula $\pi \times radius^2$ for the area of a circle, and length x width for a rectangle.)

2. Code the program for the sample task described in this chapter. Do not code the functions for Options 3 and 4. Instead, write "stubs" so that the whole program can be tested.

   If you want to use the Windows-based solution from Chapter 13, you may wish to use the InputBox function to get the file name from the user:

```
Dim FileName = InputBox("Enter new test name",
                        "Create a new test file")
```

   You will also find that the "MenuStrip" component in the "Menus & Toolbars" section of the Toolbox will be useful for building menus.

14

Chapter 15

Testing and debugging

Objectives

- Write a test plan for a program
- Test a program to detect syntax and logic errors
- Use breakpoints, stepping and the variable watch window

Drawing up a test plan

For all your programs, you need to draw up a test plan to make sure that the program will run correctly whatever the user enters. Every program that you write is likely to contain some syntax errors the first time you run it, but once you have corrected these, you need to ensure that no logic errors remain.

In this chapter you will practise debugging a program with the aid of the Visual Studio debugging tools such as breakpoints, stepping and the variable watch window.

Example 1

This program was given as an exercise in Chapter 6. The specification is as follows:

A drama group wants to record the number of tickets sold for each of their four performances. Ask the user to enter the number of tickets sold for each performance. The number must be between 0 and 120. Print an error message if an invalid number is entered, and ask them to re-enter until they enter a valid number. Print the total number of tickets sold and the average attendance for a performance.

The first task is to write a test plan. You need to test both valid and invalid entries.

- It is possible the user may accidentally type a non-numeric character. What would happen in this case?

- Test data should always include the boundary values (0 and 120 in this case), since entering data at the boundaries of legitimate values is a common source of logic errors.

- Calculate what the expected results are for valid test data.

Here is a test plan.

No.	Test purpose	Test data	Expected outcome	Actual outcome
1.	Test user input of non-numeric character	Enter choice = "asd"	Invalid choice – user asked to re-enter	
2.	Test data outside valid range for first performance	Performance 1=200 Then enter 40,80,100,90 (typical data)	Invalid data – user asked to re-enter Total = 310 Average = 77.5	
3.	Test boundary values	0, 120, 80, 40	Total = 240, Average = 60	
4.	Test data just outside boundary	-1,121,80,40 Then enter 0,120,80,40	Invalid data – user asked to re-enter after -1 and 121 entered. Total = 240, Average = 60	
5.	Test a correct entry for performance 1 followed by an incorrect entry for performance 2	Performance 1=100 Then enter 200, (not accepted),30,40,50	Total 220, Average = 55	

The version of the program shown below has logic errors in it.

```
Module Module1
    'Program name: Ch15 Example 1 with errors
    'Validates and counts tickets sold over 4 performances
```

```
        Sub Main()
            Dim total = 0
            Dim flag As Boolean
            Dim numberString As String
            Dim number As Integer
            Dim average As Double
            For performance = 1 To 4
                flag = False
                Console.Write("Please enter tickets sold for
                                performance " & performance & ": ")
                numberString = Console.ReadLine()
                While flag = False
                    Try
                        number = CInt(numberString)
                        flag = True
                    Catch ' ValueError
                        Console.WriteLine("This is not a
                                    valid number") flag = False
                    End Try

                    If flag Then
                        If number >= 0 And number < 120 Then
                            total += number
                        Else
                            Console.Write("Please re-enter
                                tickets sold for performance "
                                & performance & ": ")
                            numberString = Console.ReadLine()
                        End If
                    End If
                End While
            Next
            average = total / 4

            Console.WriteLine()
            Console.WriteLine("Total tickets sold: " & total)
            Console.WriteLine("Average number of tickets per
                                performance " & average)
            Console.WriteLine("Press Enter to exit ")
            Console.ReadLine()

        End Sub
    End Module
```

The output from Test 1 is:

```
Please enter tickets sold for performance 1: asd
This is not a valid number
This is not a valid number
This is not a valid number
This is not a valid number … (continuous loop)
```

You can terminate the program by selecting Debug, Terminate all from the menu in the development window, or by pressing the shortcut key combination Ctrl-C.

Q1 Look through the above code carefully. Why is this happening? Try and correct the error, and then try the other tests. You will find that other errors also become apparent.

Using the debugging feature

Using the debugging feature enables you to trace through each step of a program, and show the values of any variables at each step. It can be a very useful tool for finding an elusive logic error.

Example 2

This mini-tutorial uses a simple program to demonstrate how the debugger works.

1. First of all, decide where you want the tracing to start. Click in the grey margin at the left of the line numbers to set a breakpoint. The breakpoint will be indicated by a red dot.

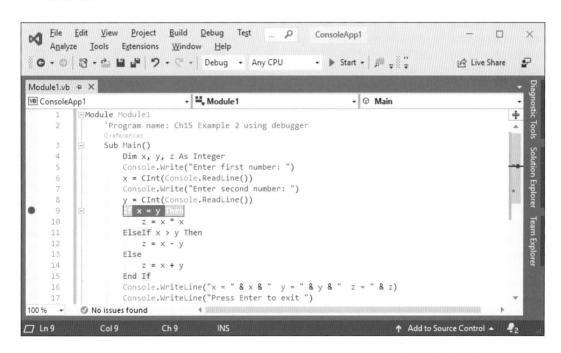

2. Now run the program. You can use the **F5** key to start execution with the debugger.

   When your program reaches the breakpoint, it will stop and display the statement that will execute next.

   You can see the variables and their current values in the **Locals** pane.

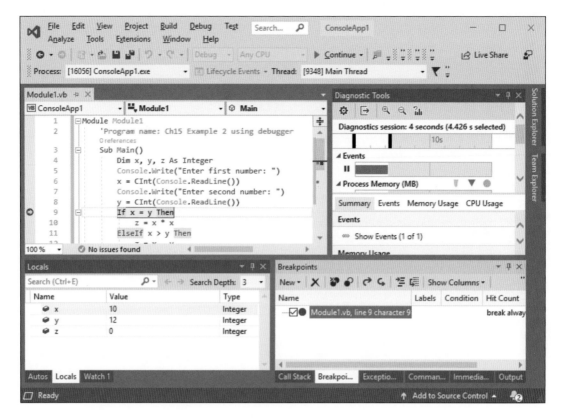

3. Press **F11** to execute the statement. The debugger will stop at the next statement. This method of executing a program is called stepping through a program.

4. At any time while stepping through the program, you can view the value of all local variables in the Locals window.

6. To stop tracing and continue running the program, press **Continue** or the **F5** key.

7. Alternatively, choose **Debug**, **Stop Debugging** (**Shift+F5**).

Exercises

1. The following program is a solution to the exercise in Chapter 6.

   Write a program to ask a user to enter a new password. The password must be between 8 and 15 characters long and have at least one lowercase letter, one uppercase letter and one numeric character. If it does not, the user should repeatedly be asked to enter a different password until they enter a valid one.

   ```
   Module Module1
       'Program name: Ch15 Exercise 1 with errors
       'validates a new password
   ```

```
Sub Main()
    Dim ucaseLetters = {"A", "B", "C", "D", "E", "F",
        "G", "H", "I", "J", "K", "L", "M", "N", "O", "P",
        "Q", "R", "S", "T", "U", "V", "W", "X", "Y", "Z"}
    Dim numbers = {"0", "1", "2", "3", "4", "5", "6",
        "7", "8", "9"}
    Dim lcaseLetters(ucaseLetters.Length - 1) As Char
    For index = 0 To ucaseLetters.Length - 1
        lcaseLetters(index) = LCase(ucaseLetters(index))
    Next
    Console.WriteLine("Your password must contain at
        least one uppercase letter one lowercase letter
        and one number. It must be between 8 and 15
        characters long")
    Console.WriteLine()
    Dim password As String
    Dim letter As String
    Dim passwordChecks = 0
    Console.Write("Please enter new password: ")
    password = Console.ReadLine()
    While passwordChecks < 3
        If Len(password) >= 8 And Len(password)
            <= 15 Then passwordChecks += 1
        End If
        For Each letter In password
            If lcaseLetters.Contains(letter) Then
                passwordChecks += 1
            End If
            If ucaseLetters.Contains(letter) Then
                passwordChecks += 1
            End If
        Next
        If passwordChecks < 3 Then
            Console.Write("Invalid password - please
                re-enter: ") password = Console.ReadLine()
            passwordChecks = 0
        End If
    End While
    Console.WriteLine("Password accepted, Press
                      Enter to exit")
    Console.ReadLine()
End Sub
End Module
```

(a) Write a test plan to thoroughly test the finished program.

(b) Harvey has written the code above, but it does not work always work correctly.
Type the code, or download it from the website **pgonline.co.uk**. (It is named Ch 15
Exercise 1 with errors.txt.) Run the tests in your test plan and fill in the actual results.

(c) Debug the program. You could use the debugging feature to help do this.

2. The following program was set as an exercise in Chapter 6. It holds an encrypted password. When the user types their password, it compares it with the stored encrypted one and if the two do not match, the user is asked to enter another password.

```
'Program name: Ch 15 Exercise 2 with errors
Module Module1
    Sub Main()
        Dim storedPassword = "EHQAB6"
        Dim passwordOK = False
        Dim password, codedPassword As String
        Dim asciiValue, codedValue As Integer
        Console.Write("Please enter your password: ")
        password = Console.ReadLine()
        While Not passwordOK
            codedPassword = ""
            For Num = 0 To Len(password) - 1
                asciiValue = Asc(password(Num))
                codedValue = asciiValue + 3
                If codedValue > Asc("X") Then
                    codedValue -= 26
                End If
                codedPassword = codedPassword +
                Chr(codedValue)
            Next
            If storedPassword = codedPassword Then
                Console.WriteLine("Password accepted")
                passwordOK = True
            Else
                Console.WriteLine("Password incorrect -
                                    re-enter: ")
            End If
        End While
        Console.WriteLine("Press Enter to exit ")
        Console.ReadLine()
    End Sub
End Module
```

(a) Write a test plan to thoroughly test the finished program.

(b) Nadia has written the above code, but it does not always work correctly. Type the code, or download it from the website **pgonline.co.uk**. (It is named Ch 15 Exercise 2 with errors.txt.) Run the tests in your test plan and fill in the actual results.

(c) Debug the program. You could use the debugging feature to help do this.

You've reached the end … congratulations!

Index